TO BE HAPPY WITHOUT MELANCHOLY , THE DOMINO EFFECT

THE GREATEST HAPPINESS COMES OUT FROM OUR GOOD ACT(READING FOR VIRTUOSO)

Kamal Kumar Prajapat

This book is dedicated to Sri Janki lal father-in-law. Thanks to Priyanka (Wife),Manika (Daughter) and Eeshan(Son) for support.

Today's busy life, there is no space for happiness but I try to understand about happiness and it is most diffi-cult than we understand and it is like moving simple to complex but without conditio sine qua non of hard work and sincere, It is not possible.

KAMAL KUMAR PRAJAPAT

CONTENTS

CHAPTERS INDEX

INTRODUCTION

This book is written in corona time. When worldwide lockdown was imposed, everyone locked in their houses. Many of them died due to depression. They could be saved but did not possible due to no contact policy or isolation, restrictions. First time, it is feel that happiness is most important and it is a weapon to fight to the depression. Books on happiness and depression are many from old time to present. This book deals for erudite who puzzled in depression, we knows everything but cannot do anything and think about why we are in depression again and again when we get into deep depression that is called domino effect, it may damage ourselves ever so. So, this book provides the common fundamental of life in depth.

This book has sixteen chapters which deals about sadness verses happiness, life motto, different type of depression, important life parameters, wellbeing, depression management, analyse with practical scenario and many more.

1.DEPRESSION

"Anything different is good."--From Groundhog Day (1993)

Depression or deep unhappiness is a common problem for human life and in a lifetime we depressed many time.Life is not easy if we think and life is easy if we take it easy.,we know very well all rules but when problem comes ,we forget the our knowledge ,strength and trap in depression.

there are many definitions of depression ,some of them are following :

1.1 Common Definition:

Sadness, feeling down or morose , and having a loss of interest or pleasure in daily activities.

Depression : it is mass noun feelings of severe despondency and dejection.

'self-doubt creeps in and that swiftly turns to depression'

Psychiatry: A mental condition characterised by feelings of severe despondency and dejection, typically also with feelings of inadequacy and guilt, often accompanied by lack of energy and disturbance of appetite and sleep.

(above definitions from https://www.lexico.com/definition/depression)

Clinical depression:A mental health disorder characterised by persistently depressed mood or loss of interest in activities, causing significant impairment in daily life.

Possible causes include a combination of biological, psychological and social sources of distress. Increasingly, these factors may cause changes in brain function and working, including mutation activity of certain neural circuits in the brain.

As per WHO survey :

- Depression is a leading cause of disability worldwide and is a major contributor to the overall global burden of disease.

- More women are affected by depression than men.

- Depression can lead to suicide.

- There are effective psychological and pharmacological treatments for moderate and severe depression.

Depression is different from usual mood fluctuations and short-lived emotional responses to challenges in everyday life. Sadness and Happiness variation with time like hours or day or month, where no equal or emotional flat or constant action has been seen, it may be normal if change not frequent otherwise we have been moving the mode of depression . Especially when long- lasting and with moderate or severe intensity, depression may become a serious health condition. It can cause the affected person to suffer greatly and function poorly at work, at school and in the family. Depression can be at its worst which lead to suicide or murder.

1.2 Depression And Anxiety

Depression and Anxiety may be related to abnormal variations in the mood and behaviour of a person. These conditions originate as a result of chemical imbalance in the brain. Most of the persons with anxiety disorders develop depression. A person suffering from depression and anxiety generally divulge feelings of contrite, incurious behaviour, low self-esteem and loss of appetency. Stress typically fade away when the stress intensity ebb with time. However, chronic stress can be auto change into instinctive anxiety or depression, so it's important to take steps to reduce or curb stress whenever likely possible.

1.3 Happiness

Generally we think that what we want if get it, I am happy otherwise sad. For whole life many time we loss and many time we get ,overall idea give if we get more than happy otherwise not happy in life.It is state of human where positive emotions at high level, mind is free from tension, heart is happy with love and emotion ,body is felling stress less .Happiness in life that effect our mind , heart, immune system. Happiness is different for different people, like for kids, toffees give happiness but not other things if they want toffees. Our wish is important for happiness and it is main root of depression .For the life moving, we shall think about new wish and change accordingly and adjust our need as wish, but if our wish is crossing the boundaries of our need, it generates uneven mood swings try to catch and solve.

2. HAPPINESS

"Real happiness in life comes from honesty and integrity"

When we talk about darkness and if we want to remove it, only light will do it similar way if we talk about depression, the happiness automatically come in to picture.

2.1 What Is Happiness?

Happiness is depending on reference and it is relative to reference. Happiness is not absolute. We compare ourselves with others and an emotion of sadness or happiness develop. It is feel by heart and our mind .When both are normal and resonant that mean we are in relax or happy. When a baby born, mother is happy and forget nine months pain. When person got as their wish or nothing work pending, just dying naturally-feel happy. When a saint sees a God in dream -feel happy. Limit of happiness cannot be limit it may be from valuable or non valuable. It may be short time or long time depends on our thoughts. Short term happiness come generally from material thing but long term happiness come only from immaterial things only. We can define immaterial thing like: visit any desire place, relationship, donation, in nature (mountain, river, trees etc), work, worship etc.

Happiness are different for different people so happiness is abstract.The absence of sadness is called happiness.Happiness effects our body chemical reaction and working of body parts.If we know what is curse ,then we can find happiness in life .

Life has many unfortunate events that effect our life it may be day to day headaches, relative problem ,our problem, kids problem ,school problem or any problem for which we think that it is problem that create tension are presence of sadness or say happiness meter down. All are depends only on our thinking and nothing more. What is life? Meaning of life is different for different people. Only motto of life is not getting happiness, even and uneven days always come together so be tranquil and take decisions from best available option and be happy always internally and destiny has other plans. Many times we try to masquerade (hiding real emotions) our self at different occasion and feel satisfied, happy.Happiness is natural feeling of happy whereas joy is for getting achievement.

Effect of sadness or tension on our body:

reacting to stress in unhealthy ways can increase your

risk of high blood pressure, heart attacks and strokes. Certain behaviours are linked to higher blood pressure, such as:

- Smoking
- Drinking too much alcohol
- Eating unhealthy foods

Also, heart disease may be linked to certain health conditions related to stress, such as:

- Anxiety
- Depression

2.2 Stress-Reducing Activities Can Lower Tension

Reducing your stress level might not directly lower tenson over the long term. But using strategies to manage your stress or tension ,can help improve your health in other ways. Mastering stress management techniques can lead to healthy behavior changes — including those that reduce your tension.

There are many options for managing stress. For example:

Simplify Our Schedule:

We can think majority of works can be classified in following tags for Important (I) and Urgent(U) works :

      a. Important but Urgent (IU)
      b.Not Important but Urgent (I'U)
      c.Important but not Urgent (IU')
      d. Not Important and not Urgent (I'U')

Priority of work preference in descanting order is IU,

I'U, IU', I'U'.

Breathe To Relax :

Breathe to relax:

following steps should follow: -

A) Preparation

-Choose a place to do our breathing exercise. It is better, should quite place and greenery.

-Try to do it once or twice a day.

-Wear comfortable clothes.

-If we have more time, we can do for 10 minutes or more to get even greater benefits.

B) Method A Deep Breathing

-We can lie on our back in bed or on the floor with a pillow under our head and knees. Or we can sit in a chair with our shoulders, head, and neck supported against the back of the chair or on the earth.

-Breathe in through our nose. Let our belly fill with air.

-Breathe out through our nose.

-Place one hand on our belly. Place the other hand on our chest.

-As we breathe in, feel our belly rise. As we breathe out, feel our belly lower. The hand on our belly should move more than the one that's on our chest.

-Take three more full, deep breaths. Breathe fully into our belly as it rises and falls with our breath.

C) Method B Breath Focus

-Close our eyes.

-Take a few big, deep breaths.

-Breathe in. As we do that, imagine that the air is filled with a sense of peace and calm. Try to feel it throughout our body.

-Breathe out. While we're doing it, imagine that the air leaves with our stress and tension.

-Now use a word or phrase with our breath. As we breathe in, say in our mind, "om namah shivay" or "I can do any thing"

-As we breathe out, say in our mind, as above.

-Continue for 15 to 30 minutes.

2.3 Mind-Wandering

Mind wandering is a spontaneous shifting of attention of thoughts from a primary task that can happen in varying degrees. It is an unintentional and unrelated shift that occurs where the mind tends to regale in varied thoughts which can disrupt the ongoing task performance.Mind wandering is another form of distraction, which can be influenced by cognitive traits (tendencies toward cognitive failure or mindful attention), states such as feeling tired or stressed, or road environment factors such as route familiarity (Burdett et al., 2016). Lack of awareness of the surrounding environment due to idée fixe (a belief that someone refuse to change) with own thoughts.

Misunderstanding during reading and listening. It is not due to lack of intelligence but rather due to mind wandering.

Inability To Focus Or Inattentive Or Day Dreaming

There is a reduced capacity to focus on the task at hand and people who allow their minds to wander may ignore what is happening around them. This can be misinterpreted as absent-mind.

Lack Of Attention

or having a short attention span in following instructions or executing a plan. They are very easily distracted from the main task at hand, and are constantly changing tasks. They continually start new tasks before finishing old ones.

Depression

A common finding in such people, this may be a consequence of mind wandering.

Sleep Disturbances

They often find it difficult to sleep at night and have irregular sleeping patterns.

Continually Losing Or Misplacing Things

due to forgetfulness & Inability to deal with stress.

Risky Behavior

Risky behavior in activities, often with little or no regard for the personal safety or the safety of others. This includes not paying attention while crossing roads, driving dangerously, an performing dangerous experiments.

start from happy and take a decision about yourself.

Indecisive Manner

It is due to person wondering mind in dithering condition & divergence.

2.4 Deliberately Dissembling

Many time wrong doing are hide from other which create unhappiness in our mind, dissonance in facial expressions & emotions.

3. DESTINY AND SUCCESS

"Success in life comes from combination of Intelligence, hard work, polite behavior, believe in yourself."

Destiny is related to degree of candour and self consciousness, it refers to individual perceptions, deliberations, cognisance, souvenirs etc if we are right minded then destiny could not be horrible.No one can change your destiny. The choice is yours. You can either accept things happily or sadly. Better to have a Happy & Positive attitude in bad times because nothing lasts forever & so holds true for bad times as well.life is a gift for us.Most of people believe that each person has his own destiny, which God gives him.

But a person during his life can change his kismet without knowing it.

From the book wings of fire:"Accept your destiny and go ahead with your life. You are not destined to become an Air Force pilot. What you are destined to

become is not revealed now but it is predetermined. Forget this failure, as it was essential to lead you to your destined path. Search, instead, for the true purpose of your existence. Become one with yourself, my son! Surrender yourself to the wish of God."
The book contains many of his own poems and his favourite poems. Here is an other example from this book,
next day Agni took off at 0710 hrs. It was a perfect launch. The missile followed a textbook trajectory. All flight parameters were met. It was like waking up to a beautiful morning from a nightmarish sleep. We had reached the launch pad after five years of continuous work at multiple work centres. We had lived through the ordeal of a series of snags in the last five weeks. We had survived pressure from everywhere to stop the whole thing. But we did it at last! It was one of the greatest moments of my life. A mere 600 seconds of elegant flight washed off our entire fatigue in an instant. What a wonderful culmination of our years of labour. I wrote in my diary that night:

Do not look at Agni
as an entity directed upward
to deter the ominous
or exhibit your might.
It is fire in the heart of an Indian.
Do not even give it
the form of a missile
as it clings to the
burning pride of this nation
and thus is bright.

I felt the paternal forces of heaven and the maternal and cosmic forces of nature embrace me as parents would hug their long-lost child. I scribbled in my diary:

Away! fond thoughts, and vex my soul no more! Work claimed my wakeful nights, my busy days Albeit brought memories of shore Yet haunt my dreaming gaze!

> We create and destroy
> And again recreate
> In forms of which no one knows.
> *AL-WAQUIAH Qur'an 56:61*

3.1 What Is Success

It can be classified as small or big. Small success in life gives big success and this process is continuous till our life.

Success means not happiness, both are totally different.All happiness are your success but vice versa not true always.

Many of us chase career titles, money, or social fame — and yet we don't feel successful when we get things.

short term success which can be achieved by short term work and move to next target by adding successes & failures of all life, we can find a point of final success but it depends to person to person.We will get future output by setting today's targets.

Success is something that you have to define for yourself, and no one can do it for you. Success could mean a sense of giving back to the world and making a difference. It could mean a sense of accomplishment and career progression.

It could mean being able to do the things you love. It could mean being able to provide the best possible up-bringing for your children.

We can't dodge our final destiny by any means.life can be saved from doom if follow simple rules of life with out any discordant for our profit.we can escape from harbinger of doom.

3.2 Sense Of Gain(SoG)

It means the quality of life , life satisfaction, fulfil basic rights, dignity and value. satisfying of needs in social life, and includes such as emotion, cognition, values, and behavioural tendencies. Income is a basic factor to measure people's quality of life. The important factor of the sense gain are sense of personal development, social security, social justice and government job satisfaction. Sense of Gain is affected by experience, environment, demography, gender, education ,social status etc.

SoG are important for present life which include multidimension parameter for quality of life.

4. WORK AREA DEPRESSION

"The root causes for chasm of abyss are Impugn of character, moral turpitude."

Every one wants to comfort & convenience but this gives lethargic effect in life so life shall not be in very comfort and convenience so we shall be busy by doing some good act.

If we drop two balls from hight ,one dropped & other hand ,one ball at the top which has maximum energy (As it can move easily if left)but lower stability,other ball at bottom which has minimum energy (can't move without push or pull) but more stability,similar way life at high success is unstable but powerful but at life end where we have no desire, life is stable.In life , we get many things providential it may be good or bad.And don't be providential,we should create prowess for ourself.All decisions should be in prudence & act accordingly.

In unhappiness situation human mind struct into about God existence, he is est or non-est.Bleak time shall be forgotten as nightmare otherwise we will struct in nihilism.For any work situations should not become in angry if not controlled than feel sorry & promise not to do again.Our memories go in nostalgic memories, suddenly come in present but feel, it is sad.It is good to roam into nostalgia but more than limit, it is harmful to ourselves.

Divergent of information by divulging, is generally may create a dodge or dizzy & starting mind wondering.

Poor project practices. This may result in miscommunication, missed deadlines, blown budgets, or products that miss the mark. People want to be on a winning team that produces good work, but barriers to accomplishing this can contribute to depression.Let's examine some causes.

4.1 Wrong Fit Position

When we are doing work ,where we should not to be.It is like a engineer doing a work of clerk or a doctor doing administrative job.

4.2 Less Salary In Job

When we are getting less salary for our job comparing salary with others who are getting more salary.

4.3 Overburden Or Very Less Work

When work load is more than our capacity or very less than our capacity.

Value to dishonest person :Many time in work area, dishonest person grow fast than honest.

Ethical discomfort or dilemma:Our ethical values confront with company working style.

Miscommunication :When information not communicate as it is received or convey the information not with full required data or information.

Disinformation :convey false information and act accordingly.

4.4 Poor Working Condition

When working condition at work place not as per our choice or desire.

4.5 No Faithful Environment Available

The person with moral turpitude or doubtful identity may create dubious environment at work.

4.6 Less Work Knowledge

The less work knowledge or hide information back to door may create problem.

4.7 Bullying At Work

Bullying behaviours faced in the workplace can be a huge problem for some employees, whether they're bullied by bosses, co-workers or clients.

4.7 Low Morale Or Low Engagement At Work

This may happen due to the way a company spins information rather than being transparent, puts blame for leadership mistakes on others, nickel-and-dimes employees in the name of cost containment, and rewards ineffective managers.

4.8 Poor Working Conditions

There are many conditions that become problematic when management will not take corrective action, for example, not letting employees take enough breaks, or ignoring safety concerns and temperature discomfort

4.9 Other Factor:

Unhappiness in personal life also may create problem ,reasons may be domestic violence ,financial position,alcoholic habit, hot talk in family member or self,Your status in family and friends,women/men education and thinking.Others factor that create unhappiness in life are wealth and family prospects, socioeconomic, dreams,contradiction / confrontation,confusion,love and sex in life, negative thought, consciousness, human quality, corruption in system,social status.

5.ELEMENT OF LIFE AND AFFECT

"Whether you believe in theist or non-theist or else Agnostic, you are the only one who can act according yourself so believe on yourself."

ɪngénue may be good in life or may be bad but you will not be impecunious, completely innocuous in all. We are moving with problems & solving but in wrong way, problems are not down but looming & lose our head. The lugubrious mood increasing when our beloved left us, think that life become loom but be forbear to do something act like loathe or lunatic. It is difficult to know louche personality first time but can be understand slowly. Such person contact shall be avoidable. Many time lurking by our knowing persons are done and can't do anything. If those are not left, we stuck in maelstrom. Due to accident or natural, maimed for life by some reason for deep depression but we should accept reality & move forward to work hard. If our ethical or unethically does not seen by anyone per se it is important think about self that it is wrong or right. Any action or work shall not being done as perfunctory way. We can't put a perjury for ourself for our act where we are our judge otherwise it is perpetrate act & can't do for perpetually. Majestic, regal life may not give you happiness. We shall not be in status of malice. If feel manic, frenzied frequently shall think about the reason. We should happy what we have. Sometimes we are in state of perplexed but perspicacious of problem is key tool to solve.

True purpose of life :

- Why are we here? or What are we here for?
- What is the origin of life?
- What is the nature of life? What is the nature of reality?

- What is the purpose of life? What is the purpose of one's life?
- What is the significance of life?
- What is meaningful and valuable in life?
- What is the value of life?
- What is the reason to live? What are we living for?

5.1 Element Of Body :

As per old belief we belief about elements of body are:water ,air,earth,fire,sky.

As per wikipedia (https://en.m.wikipedia.org/wiki/Cremation),Cremation leaves behind an average of 2.4 kg (5.3 lbs) of remains, known as "ashes" or "cremains".Cremated remains are mostly dry calcium phosphates with some minor minerals, such as salts of sodium and potassium. Sulphur and most carbon are driven off as oxidised gases during the process, although about 1% -4% of carbon remains as carbonate. the main elements are calcium,Phosphorus,Oxygen. Other parameters that effect human body are ambient temperature and sun rays and body temperature, humidity, sleep.

When relax in life less or high than less depression or may be high depression wise versa so the state totally depend on us.for existence of life work ,unhappiness both are part of life it is like unhappiness is nothing but only absence of happiness.

Water

Human body is consumed water that give hydration to human body. Amount of consumption of water can affect mental & physical ability.The water mineral affect our thinking ability and physical efficiency.So we should drink sufficient water that body needs.

India consider the river Ganges an embodiment of the goddess Ganga. This makes the Ganges River both a symbol of life and a place where one can wash away spiritual impurities, thereby drawing closer to the sacred source of life.

In the creation story of the Jewish Torah and Christian Bible, God's spirit first moved"over the face of the waters" and God said "Let the waters bring forth swarms of living creatures" (Genesis 1:2, 20). In Islam, water is the origin of all life on Earth. The Qur'an says water is the substance from which God created the human being (25:54). At creation, even God's throne "was upon water" (11:7).

Air

We should take fresh air for healthy body.Plantation is the only way that we get fresh air, our mental health will be healthy if we get more fresh air from plants. Plants are natural air filter.

5.2 The Dilemma In Life

The trolley problem is a series of thought experiments in ethics and psychology, involving stylized ethical dilemmas of whether to sacrifice one person to save a larger number.You have two options:

1.   Do nothing and allow the trolley to kill the five people on the main track.
2.   Pull the lever, diverting the trolley onto the side track where it will kill one person.

Which is the more ethical option? Or, more simply: What is the right thing to do?

A dilemma is a problem offering two possibilities, neither of which is unambiguously acceptable or preferable. The possibilities are termed the horns of the dilemma, a clichéd usage, but distinguishing the dilemma from other kinds of predicament as a matter of usage.the dilemma constitutes a false dichotomy, that is, a fallacy. Traditional usage distinguished the dilemma as a "horned syllogism" from the sophism that attracted the Latin name cornutus.

5.3 Money Power Fame

Do not chase money, fame, power and pleasure:

Money: Money is required for many things in lives.Every one work for money but we should not left our ethics ,integrity, honesty.

Fame: Fame is with high wealthy person, who hard work to maintain a fame.So work hard is key to get fame in life.Fame is not necessary that all world should know you ,small success at small village can get fame in village.Always do work hard continuously whether you are star or dim.

Power: It is human tendency to enjoy privilege but when we are not getting that privilege ,then what does we think and we tried or think some negative in mind so left all privilege and be polite always.

Pleasure: Life is spent with all pleasure and human try to get but it is not life long so try to leave in every type of condition.

5.4 Behaviour And Decision

In exasperation, we know what we are doing but in apoplectic, we are not in control of ourselves.

Apoplectic, furious & angry - Every species has some point of tolerance but after that emotions blast in the form of angry or furious, apoplectic.For human being angriness is common, but furiously act when got stimuli to limit of respects. It exacerbate the problem and enter in state of depression and apoplectic will blocked your thinking, doing the action which can be not good or trauma for you.

your loves one has important position to control your apoplectic or may increase this.

5.5 SWOT Analysis Of Ourselves

SWOT refers as

S-Strength,W-Weakness ,O:Opportunities,T-Threats decisions according to SWOT will help and save in unnecessary trouble in life.

We should think our capabilities according to strength,weakness,opportunities,threats and go ahead.

We should flagellate and get up to kick against the pricks i.e we should not punish ourself and who give harm ,kick them from our life.

We might define character as a commitment to do what is wise, honest and right, regardless of the cost or circumstances. For example, a person of good character will not steal or cheat, even in times of great need. A person of good character will speak the truth even if there is a price to pay for doing so. A person of good character will show courage even when the cause appears to be lost.You can be a person of exceptional character even if you do not have exceptional talent, intellect, skills or education.

5.6 Good Character

It is something anyone can develop. Character consists of:

1. Integrity:

Interity may be defined as a pattern of consistency and congruence between your words and your actions. A person of authentic character and integrity will behave in exactly the same way, whether he or she is in public or in private. That person's behavior will be just as honourable, ethical and moral when no one is watching as when he or she is being observed by others.

2. Honesty:

People of honesty are sincere, genuine and committed to living with truth. Honest people admit their mistakes and refuse to cut ethical corners.It also means being honest with yourself. You can't lie to yourself and pretend that everything is all right when it isn't. You have to address your destructive behavior, your wrong attitudes, your character flaws.

3. Humility:

Humility means to understand who you really are – a child of God. Then you do not have any ego, nor are you inflated by pleasure and deflated by criticism. They do not worry about what others think.

4. Responsibility:

Responsible people are self-starters. No one has to stand over them with a whip to make sure they get their work done. They take their duties seriously and carry them out without having to be monitored. Responsible people also take personal responsibility for their own actions. If they make a mistake, they don't make excuses or shift the blame to others. They own up to their mistakes—and correct them. They hold themselves accountable for their own actions.

5. Compassion:

People of compassion show kindness, mercy and benevolence to all people, regardless of any distinctions. Genuine compassion does not arise from the emotions, but from an act of the will—a conscious and volitional decision to do good to other people. Compassionate people willingly sacrifice their own comfort and

6. Courage:

Courage is the willingness to take risks to achieve great goals, the willingness to withstand opposition and face obstacles for a great cause, and the willingness to face suffering and death with dignity in order to set an example of character for others to follow.

7. Love:

It is absent of abhorrent.The degree of love is changed only for different event or relation.Absent of love may be accepted but long time abhorrent,invoke noxious are not good.We can move with novice but not with noxious think or abhorrent act or repugnant behaviour.

5.7 Influence

Acquiring fortune, achieving fame, pursuing power, chasing pleasure—if these are your life goals, my friend, then you are busily frittering away your life. Why waste your life on such meaningless goals when you could invest your life in making a lasting difference in the lives of others and in the world around you? Some practical ways by which you can have influence on the world around you are:

- Be careful of what you say
- Always be positive.(B+)
- Get achievements that influence to inspire the next generation. (IG)
- Optimise use of your time and resources.
- Ethics and integrity are above the personal advantage.
- Ask yourself: Is it legal? Is it logical?

5.8 Parenthood

There are many ways to "pursue parenthood." A "parent" could be a birth parent, a step-parent, an adoptive parent, a grandparent, a godparent, an aunt or uncle, a parental figure like a coach or mentor, or anyone else with the capacity to love and nurture a young person. So even if you never have birth children of your own, you can pursue parenthood. Some practical ways to do this are:

Give Kids The Gift Of Your Time:

When you spend time with your kids, you show them they are important to you and that you value them. Take time to talk to them, look them in the eye, listen to them, hug them, play games with them, share meals with them, help them with their homework, guide them and affirm them. Enjoy maximum time with family & kids as possible as.

Affirm Unstintingly:

Always convey unconditional acceptance and affirmation of youngsters, whether they win or lose, succeed or fail. Even if the child doesn't perform as well as you'd hoped, never let your disappointment show. If you only affirm and praise a kid when he succeeds, he'll sense that your acceptance is conditional—and when he fails, he'll feel condemned and devalued.We need to tell them, regardless of their performance, "I'm proud of you. I believe in you. I'm on your side whether you make a touchdown or a fumble, whether you break the tape or finish last." We are their balcony people, and we affirm them simply because they are here.

Listen To Your Kids

Stop, look and listen: That's shorthand for "Stop what you're doing, look your kids in the eye and listen to what they're really saying to you." All too often, we pretend that we are listening to our kids, but we are really just waiting for the interruption to be over. We say, "Uh-huh… . Yeah… . That's nice." And we don't hear a word they're saying. Kids aren't stupid. They know when they're being patronised—and being patronised makes them feel devalued and unimportant. Listen for what kids don't say. We need to listen to our kids 'feelings, not just their words. We need to give them permission to express their fears, hurts and other emotions, and let them know that their feelings will be heard and accepted.

Focus on being real, not perfect: We parents make mistakes. When we do, kids know it. So when you mess up, 'fess up(""Confession is good for the soul." – Scottish Proverb"). Admit that you were wrong and ask forgiveness. Many parents seem to feel that saying "I'm sorry" to their children will cause them to be diminished in their kids 'eyes. Not so! Your kids need to see that you are big enough to admit mistakes—and by doing so, you set a good example.

Be consistent and dependable: When we keep our promises, we build a sense of security in our kids' lives. When we are consistent and dependable, kids know they can expect us to keep our word—and to follow through on our warnings.

Set A Good Example

One of the most important duties you have as a parent (or parent substitute) is to be an inspirational role model for that child. Remember, those kids are watching your every move. They are learning what it means to be a responsible and effective adult by watching how you live your life. They are checking to see if what you say matches what you do. When you make ethical decisions and respond to pressures and crises, they are taking mental notes and filing them away for future reference.

Encourage kids to invest their lives in what truly matters: As you.

5.9 Faith

God loves you and has a wonderful plan for your life. Ignorance separates us from God and hence we cannot understand that. The Divine is the only thing that will satisfy us and the key thing we have to do is to surrender to Him.Every human being ever born is made in God's image and created for a purpose. God doesn't make mistakes. The circumstances of your birth and childhood don't matter. You are here because God put you here, and the world needs you. This is your one and only irreplaceable life, and God has called you to carry out His eternal purpose for your life. God has gifted you and provided you with passions, talents and abilities that can make a lasting difference in the world. To develop faith, do the following:

Study Religious Books:

the Bhagavad Gita, the Bible, etc. When you study them, study with humility, trying to apply the teachings to your own life. Everyone of us is a child of God. We all have our own roles. The most important thing is to show up.

Pray

Pray in simple words whatever you want, feel or need to express. Sing his songs and mantras.Face adversity in reliance upon God. My friend, don't waste your life chasing after money, fame, power or pleasure. The meaning of your life can only be found by answering God's call upon your life, by joining your finite life to

His infinite and eternal life, and by immersing yourself in prayer and His Word. Connect your heart to His, and He will lead you safely through this life and into the life that never ends.

5.10 Money Vs Happiness Vs Depression: Money Can't Buy Happiness'

According to the Origins of Happiness report, eliminating mental health issues such as depression and anxiety would increase happiness by 20%, whereas eliminating poverty would increase happiness by only 5%. In other words, tackling mental health problems would be four times more effective at increasing happiness than reducing poverty. And the best part, say the researchers behind the report is that reducing mental illness doesn't have to cost a penny.

If you have good mental wellbeing (or good mental health), you are able to:

- feel relatively confident in yourself – you value and accept yourself and judge yourself on realistic and reasonable standards

- feel and express a range of emotions

- feel engaged with the world around you – you can build and maintain positive relationships with other people and feel you can contribute to the community you live in

- live and work productively

- cope with the stresses of daily life and manage times of change and uncertainty.

5.11 Resilience

Resilient people are able to utilise their skills and strengths to cope and recover from problems and challenges.Resilience does not eliminate stress or erase life's difficulties. People who possess this resilience don't see life through rose-colored lenses. They understand that setbacks happen and that sometimes life is hard and painful. They still experience the emotional pain, grief, and sense of loss that comes after a tragedy, but their mental outlook allows them to work through such feelings and recover.

Instead, resilience gives people the strength to tackle problems head-on, overcome adversity, and move on with their lives.

Focusing on the positive things you can do can help get you out of a negative mindset.

Resilience is evident when a one's health and development tips toward positive outcomes — even when a heavy load of factors is stacked on the negative outcome side.

The single most common factor for one who develop resilience is at least one stable and committed relationship with a supportive parent, caregiver, or other adult.

Resilience improved by practical life Experience and try to hope of learn.They always learn from life and hardships of life.

5.12 Look After Your Physical Health

If you have good physical health, you are more likely to have good mental health. Sleep patterns, diet and physical activity all have an impact on your mental wellbeing.

Sleep

If you have trouble sleeping, this can have a serious impact on your mental wellbeing. Negative feelings are likely to be exaggerated and you might find you are more irritable and less confident. (See Mind's booklet How to cope with sleep problems for help with establishing a good sleep routine.)

Diet(If Eat Good Then Think Good)

Eating healthily has a positive impact on your physical and mental health. Eating a well-balanced diet at regular meal-times with plenty of water and vegetables will help you to feel more healthy and happy. Stopping or reducing your alcohol intake, and avoiding tobacco and recreational drugs can also help improve your general wellbeing.

Physical Activity

Physical activity is good for mental health, particularly if you exercise outdoors. Being active can help reduce depression and anxiety and boost your self-confidence. It also releases endorphins ' –feel-good 'hormones that can help improve your mood. It doesn't matter whether you prefer

5.13 Do Something You Enjoy

Doing something you enjoy can improve your confidence and help you stay well. Make time to do things you like, whether it's cooking, seeing your friends or doing DIY(doing it yourself). Some people find that doing something creative, such as drama, drawing or sewing, helps them to express themselves positively and deal with any difficult emotions in a positive way. Composing and playing music helps me express feelings that are difficult to explain in words.

Learning something new, or taking up a new hobby, can also boost your confidence and occupies your mind in a positive and active way. If you want to try a new hobby, think about what you are good at, or things that you have always wanted to try. You can find information about volunteering organisations and local groups, clubs or classes at your local library, in local newspapers or magazines, or online.

for eg:

- Solve maths problems :sudoku problem, counting triangle etc
- Making art or creative art
- Writing Books
- Talking more or less
- Let's do dance
- Do joking, running, yoga, meditation etc
- Sing a song
- Play games

5.14 Do Something For Someone Else

Doing something for someone else, such as helping a friend or relative with their chores or volunteering for a charity, has been shown to have a positive impact on mental wellbeing. It can help you improve your self-confidence and meet new people, and makes you feel that you are making a positive contribution to your community. (See 'Useful contacts' on p. 21 for information about volunteering opportunities in your area.)

5.15 Set Yourself A Challenge

Set yourself a challenge that you can realistically achieve. This doesn't have to be anything particularly large but should have meaning for you.

5.16 Relax

It's important to make time to relax, even if you don't feel under stress. This may mean going away for the weekend, spending an evening doing something you like, or even just taking a five-minute break to look out of the window. Learning a relaxation technique, such as breathing exercises, yoga or meditation, can also help you relax and reduce stress levels.

Relaxation is not the same as recreation. Hobbies and other activities can become stressful if they become excessive.

5.17 Identify Mood Triggers

Keeping track of your moods in a mood diary can help you work out what affects your mental wellbeing and recognise changes in your mood that would be difficult to spot otherwise. For example, you may realise that eating certain foods or seeing a certain person has an effect on your mood. Or you may tend to experience a particular mood at a particular time, such as before your period or in winter.

Knowing what affects your moods can help you take

steps to avoid or change the situations that have a negative impact on you. Even if you can't change the situation, knowing your triggers can help you remember to take extra care of yourself during difficult times.

You can create your own mood diary, or there are lots to choose from on the internet Everyone has times when they face challenging situations and find it difficult to cope. If you are experiencing a difficult time, or are unwell, it's important to look after yourself and try and get through.

Be careful not to put too much pressure on yourself to carry on as normal. You may need to take a break from your usual responsibilities, for example reducing your social activities or workload. Take small steps and don't expect too much of yourself. Try to get enough sleep and eat regularly. If you are finding it difficult to cope on your own, don't be afraid to ask for help. For example, you may need time off work or help with day-to-day tasks, such as cleaning or childcare.

5.18 Learn To Accept Yourself

The more I am at peace with myself and who I am, the more I am likely to be at peace with others and who they are.

One of the most important steps in staying mentally healthy is to learn to accept yourself. If you value yourself, you are more likely to have positive relationships with other people and find it easier to cope with difficult times in your life.

Here are some tips to help you increase your self-esteem (also see Mind's booklet How to increase your self-esteem):

• Try not to compare yourself to other people.

• Don't strive for perfection.

• Acknowledge your positive qualities and things you are good at.

• Learn to identify and challenge unhelpful thinking patterns.

• Use self-help books and websites to help you change your beliefs.

• Spend time with supportive people.

• Be assertive – don't allow people to treat you with a lack of respect.

• Engage in work and hobbies that you enjoy.

What helped me was the realisation that this is who I am, to stop fighting it and realise that life may not be what you expected it to be... Then, just start living again.

• Positive Emotions (developing a playlist to have more enjoyment in life)

• Engagement (getting into flow and playing to your

strengths)

- Relationships (nurturing your interpersonal well-being)

- Meaning (finding meaning and purpose in life)

- Achievement (setting goals to build your future house of happiness)

5.19 Manage Your Stress Levels

If you have a lot of stress in your life, find ways to reduce it, such as learning a few time-management techniques.

Introduce regular exercise and time to yourself. These are positive changes. Taking control of your time in this way can effectively reduce stress.

If you have feelings of anxiety along with your stress, breathing techniques can help. Try breathing exercise for stress.Enjoy yourself

Doing things that you enjoy is good for your emotional wellbeing.

Simple activities like watching sports with a friend, having a soak in the bath or meeting up with friends for coffee can all improve your day.Doing something you're good at, such as cooking or dancing, is a good way to enjoy yourself and have a sense of achievement.

Try to avoid things that seem enjoyable at the time but make you feel worse afterwards, such as drinking too much alcohol or eating junk food.

5.20 Boost Your Self-Esteem

Self-esteem is the way you feel about yourself.

The best way to improve your self-esteem is to treat yourself as you'd treat a valued friend, in a positive but honest way.

Notice when you're putting yourself down, such as thinking, "You're so stupid for not getting that job", and instead think, "Would I say that to my best friend?". You probably wouldn't.

Tell yourself something positive instead, such as: "You're a bright person, you'll get the next job".

Have a healthy lifestyle

Limit your alcohol intakeWhen times are hard, it's tempting to drink alcohol because it "numbs" painful feelings.

But it can exaggerate some feelings and make you feel angry or aggressive. It can also make you feel more depressed.

Build your resilienceResilience is what allows you to cope with life's ups and downs.

Making something worthwhile out of painful times helps your resilience grow.

Starting a support group to help others, or making something creative out of bad experiences by, for example, writing, painting or singing, can help you express pain and get through hard times.

5.21 Debt Trap

Debt trap should not be avoided and dont struck in greedy offer.No debt shall be ideal for happy life. Debt and stress are like co-joined twins.Anger As the economy sagged, anger issues rose. The phenomenon got its own name in medical circles: Debt-Anger Syndrome.

A scream in mountain or in lonely may give you release from depression.

5.22 Treadmill Effect

The hedonic treadmill, also known as hedonic adaptation, is the observed tendency of humans to quickly return to a relatively stable level of happiness despite major positive or negative events or life changes.According to this theory, as a person makes more money, expectations and desires rise in tandem, which results in no permanent gain in happiness. Philip Brickman and Donald T. Campbell coined the term in their essay "Hedonic Relativism and Planning the Good Society" (1971).The concept dates back centuries, to such writers as St. Augustine, cited in Robert Burton's 1621 Anatomy of Melancholy: "A true saying it is, Desire hath no rest, is infinite in itself, endless, and as one calls it, a perpetual rack, or horse-mill."

6.BASIC PERSONAL ELEMENT

"Practice truth is a real an ascetic's penance. "

There are few important personal Element and truth which give the way to out of any trouble .Basic element of human are traits or quality of any human being and identify the person. :

- Common sense
- Attitudes
- Truthfulness
- honest
- Emphathy
- Resilience
- Irk

6.1 Common Sense

Common sense is sound and prudent judgment based on a simple perception of the situation or facts and ability to reach appropriate conclusions. It is not a special study but rather an experience and logical thought and consciousness about near things .We can say for any small action, we should ask some question from ourselves:

1. Should I do it?

2. Why am doing this?

3. Why does should do?

4. Is any loss if fail to do?

5. What are requirements?

6. What are different ways to do?

7. Have complete the task?

8. Is more action required?

Our surrounding, we can see that common sense is not common and we have to explain the action always and many times. So Common sense is not common, if you have it than you are a genius. Every time common sense has many other elements for decision and experience. If we are learning from our fault it means our common sense is improving and vice versa.

Common sense always come from our fault and if we are doing nothing than common sense will be nothing. We should aware about surrounding and decision shall be logical than outcome will not abstract.

Common sense of person does not depend on qualification rather than an experience.
Some common sense fundamental:
1) All are equal.
2) All need food to live.
3) 2+2=4
4) One question has many ways to answer and vice versa.
5) Unethical or wrong acts have punishment.
6) Any thing in world has some value which can be in any form.
7) Destiny is common for all but the ways are different to reach destiny.
8) Every action has a reaction.
9) Every one has some mind.

6.2 Attitudes

The Attitudes is the way of thinking and behavior. It has mainly three parts that are cognitive thought, emotional thinking, and type of Behavior.

Cognition :

Cognition is the mental processes involved in gaining knowledge and perception of atmosphere and include thinking, knowing, remembering, judging, and problem-solving ability, language, imagination, perception, and planning, emotion.

Emotional Thinking:

Our thoughts control our feelings and behavior it vice versa also right. Feeling can control our thought and similar way our behavior and for others also.Emotional thinking: Our thoughts control our feelings and behavior it vice versa also right. Feeling can control our thought and similar way our behavior and for others also. Emotion may be touch with interest field, family, friends, subject, money etc. Suppressing of emotions in any incident or event that may be controlled only by our thoughts.

Behavior:

 Appropriate behavior for at apt situation is important. It should be desirable that understand the real situation and behave like way. Our behavior shall be resonant with body language or face expression. But many times illogical behavior expected from us, so our mind should be opened and think for benefit of human kind, weight it with logic and science.

Attitude may be positive (+ve), negative(-ve) and neutral they can be one step higher like very +ve, very –ve.Some times very +ve or very –ve can create problems.+ve person may be optimistic .We should be +ve attitude always.

Positive Attitude

This type of attitude is comprised of the following things;

- Confidence and optimism.

- Happy and cheerful.

- Sincerity.

- Sense of responsibility.

- They remain flexible in their approach.Some solutions always available of problem and think to solve.

- Determined in their tasks.

- They are the most Reliable persons.

- On account of their flexibility, they remain Willing to adapt according to the new challenges and situations.

- Normal life style but not high in moral.

- Such persons exercise great degree of diligence.

We can improve our attitude by education, facing real life problem, by social discussion or by gathering or induction of good people.

6.3 Truthfulness*

Truthfulness means to speak the truth habitually. A truthful man will never tell a lie. He always says what he means.

6.4 Honest*

Honesty - a moral character of a human being, related

to telling the truth.There is no mix of untrue and true. There is no mix of untrue and true. Trueness is present in blood; it cannot be learnt from books but may be developed from experience and life problem.We can say "honesty is the best policy".

6.5 Empathy

One who understand & feel the emotions other's. But it is not easy it requires extra mind and experience for which one who pass-through from such similar situation, we can compare with helpful tendencies, welfare or pro-social. Empathy in human can be developed by training or reading or by experience. It helps in individuals to equate with others. We should be motivated and train our minds to become more loving and caring.

6.6 Resilience

Resilience is the capacity to recover or to bear from difficult life situation.In life evry one face many difficult situation and clear the problem but many of them has been broken due to not able to bear situation.
diligence:it is carefulness and persistent effort or work.
Due diligence is expected diligence when one owes a responsibility of the other.
For success in life diligence and due diligence important part of life.

6.7 Irk

Irk is the basic emotion which reasoned to someone. The act that we don't like, initiate first step of irk. High intensity of irk convert in anger. So, we should control the cause of irk. First identify reasons then solutions. You are only can solve your problem and no one help.In real life ,same problem has many solution and similar way same solution for the same problem is not possible or vice versa.

 *There are exception in real world that are not right but ethical.

7.FAILURE

"All people everywhere are human beings and deserve to be treated like humans."

Failure is the state or condition of not meeting a desirable or intended objective or task, and may be viewed as the opposite of success. [The criteria for failure depends on context, and may be relative to a particular observer or belief system. One person might consider a failure what another person considers a success, particularly in cases of direct competition (or a zero-sum game). Similarly, the degree of success or failure in a situation may be differently viewed by person to person , such that a situation that one considers to be a failure, another might consider to be a success, a qualified success or a neutral situation.

When we hurt someone which is wrong ethically ,same pang reach inside us.

When action is negative, output is negative or vice versa or nothing then ex nihilo nihil fit (Nothing comes from nothing) so action has always important for our future.

If action occurred without your involvement like creatio ex nihilo(matter is not eternal but had to be created by some divine creative act) then accept, it is God & you will be look after.

7.1 Zero-Sum Games

Correlations are always inverse; there is always a winner and a loser.our happiness only from other lose or from other feel bed

by proportional happiness, loss of other or bed feeling of other.

7.2 Non-Zero-Sum Games

 Correlations are joined. Win/Win or Lose/Lose situation.

sadness is related to loss of other or bed feeling of other.loss of other or bed feeling of other increase than happiness increased or viceversa.

covetousness :eager or excessive desire, especially for wealth or possessions.

> *"As covetousness is the root of all evil, so poverty*
> *is the worst of all snares."Daniel Defoe*

Greed, also known as avarice, cupidity or covetousness, is the inordinate desire to possess wealth, goods, or objects of abstract value with the intention to keep it for one's self, far beyond the dictates of basic survival and comfort. It is applied to a markedly high desire for and pursuit of wealth, status, and power.

From Bible:-Exodus 20:17("Thou shall not covet")
"You shall not covet your neighbor's house; you shall not covet your neighbor's wife or his male servant or his female servant or his ox or his donkey or anything that belongs to your neighbor."

7.3 Naive Cynicism

Naive cynicism is the belief that individuals expect other people's judgement will consistently be motivated by their their own self-interest and that others will always view themselves in the most flattering light available. These beliefs are held while believing that one's own judgement and motivations are beyond questions or suspicion. This point of view should be tempered by the knowledge that there are other unselfish people who are motivated by the interests of others rather than their own and not everyone in an egotist who believes in their own perfection.In a related quote, Joel Feinberg, in his 1958 paper "Psychological Egoism", embraces a similar critique by drawing attention to the infinite regress of psychological egoism:

"All men desire only satisfaction."
"Satisfaction of what?"
"Satisfaction of their desires."
"Their desires for what?"
"Their desires for satisfaction."
"Satisfaction of what?"
"Their desires."
"For what?"
"For satisfaction"—etc., ad infinitum

Evocative good memory & bad memory which give strength to your mind.life is beyond zero sum game.

7.4 Real Truth

The real truth of life is death. Death is the ultimate defeat. No matter how many successes we have, we are all doomed to suffer the final failure.

Identify wrong act or person:
- Non resonant in act and say.
- May be very polite or aggressive.
- Unreasonable talk.
- Showing /manipulating things.
- Taking keen interest where is no requirement of such act.
- Mixing false statements with true statements.

Relate your sadness to others, relatively happy or sad. you are always in between sadness and happiness if compare to other and that is our real problem. In real life, an imaginary factor always will change ourselves so every think is in our mind. Human behaviour is not linear with time, it is affected and changed by many external and internal factors, we can say in mathematical final output of life is zero always be true but cross many even and uneven events in life also initially condition always important for solution of human life.

7.5 Life Decisions

Life decisions shall be considered following parameters: ethos (ethics or credibility), pathos (Emotion), logos(logic) Ethos -it means a set of belief idea etc. about social behaviour and relationship. Many times, it is contradiction with logos (logic) & some time with pathos (emotion), Balance with all shall be in life, it is not that logos further more than enough or ethos or pathos. Some time we had to forget logic & move to pathos like watching comedy movies and we are happy. We have a reminiscent look when we see things that are attached with us, it is good to remember old but not flow with bad or good reminiscent be present today & target for next when achieve one goal take energy from old good or bad reminiscent. If we hurt by torment and if we are not against it then it is totally loss full for our life so come ahead against any torment but follow SWOT analysis and loss/profit and watch the situation.

7.6 IKIGAI

IKIGAI is a Japanese concept that means your 'reason for being.' 'Iki' in Japanese means 'life,' and 'gai' describes value or worth. Your IKIGAI is your life purpose or your bliss.

What is the meaning of my life?Is the point just to live longer, or should I seek a higher purpose?

Happiness is inside us,we should search inside.There is no term like retire.

7.6 The 80 Percent Secret

80% of results flow from 20% of causes, Fill your belly to 80 percent. In life 80% problem come from 20% people or 80% success only come from your 20% effort. We use only 20% mind to get 80% success in life.

If you are busy, definitely you will be happy. "If you

keep your mind and body busy, you'll be have long life and happy."

7.7 SFOF Technique:

S-simplicity in living

F-Fight for your self

O-Optimistic for life

F-(Every think is fine)Every think that is going or gone is good for me.

Simplicity and optimise thought ,think in positive way are key success in life.

8.HABITS ,FOOD AND US

"Only we are responsible for our act ,nothing one else"

Our habits and food, what we eat that give us positive energy. Good habits and good food are the key piler of thought and health. What time, what we should eat that is complicate idea but what we eat are important.

8.1 Habits

Every one face bad things in life and fingerprints in our mind .forget bad(that will effect our Prefrontal Cortex) by following methods may help:

1)create positive image in mind and positive moving picture.

2)take proper sleep(but not disturb sleep cycle) .

3)watch happy movement or comedy

4)Engage in sports, dance, yoga or any interested activity.

5)thanks to all acts, happy wishes to others.

6)hug with love one

7)Make drawing, cartoons with written comments.

8)Do volunteer job or donate ,service to others
9)learn and solve puzzle
10)Make new relation
11)Exercise(running etc)
14)Music as like

Everyone is doing work for pecuniary gain but it should not from unethical or illegal or illegitimate way.Many times, we learn or expertise in field the field & become specialists of particular area but we don't know ,when we become pedant, start a new terrific or irksome life, It gives result after a year or long time so don't become pedant, be logical & expert.

Help of human kind in any form shall be pro bono, like educational, charity, legal. Our act are good , logical explain pro se to God or to responsible.

Pending work shall not in state of procrastination otherwise serious result will come out.

We should come out from procrastination & blaming game.

Perfectionism:It may affect if doing in negative way.

Poor posture-good posture can increase positive attitude.

Our mind is like pegasus which moving any where & making new pegasus dream.Unknowingly we used pejorative statements against other at later time we feel it so whenever we feel, say sorry or feel penance every work that we are doing, shall be with penchant otherwise we won't be successful.

8.2 A View About Some Nutrition And Superfood

Serotonin

Serotonin has a wide variety of functions in the human body. People sometimes call it the happy chemical, because it contributes to well-being and happiness.The scientific name for serotonin is 5-hydroxytryptamine (5-HT). It is mainly present in the brain, bowels, and blood platelets. Serotonin is a neurotransmitter, and some also consider it a hormone. The body uses it to send messages between nerve cells. It appears to play a role in mood, emotions, appetite, and digestion. As the precursor for melatonin, it helps regulate sleep-wake cycles and the body clock.

Tryptophan

Tryptophan plays a role in the production of serotonin, a mood stabiliser, melatonin, which helps regulate sleep patterns, niacin or vitamin B-3, and nicotinamide also known as vitamin B-6.Tryptophan has the lowest concentration in the body of any amino acid, yet, it is vital for a wide variety of metabolic functions that affect your mood, cognition, and behavior

Norepinephrine

Norepinephrine also called noradrenaline is both a hormone, produced by the adrenal glands, and a neurotransmitter, a chemical messenger which transmits signals across nerve endings in the body. Norepinephrine is produced in the inner part of the adrenal glands, also called the adrenal medulla.

Dopamine :

Dopamine is a chemical found naturally in the human body. It is a neurotransmitter, meaning it sends signals from the body to the brain. Dopamine plays a part in controlling the movements a person makes, as well as their emotional responses. The right balance of dopamine is vital for both physical and mental wellbeing.

Vital brain functions that affect mood, sleep, memory, learning, concentration, and motor control are influenced by the levels of dopamine in a person's body. A dopamine deficiency may be related to certain medical conditions.

8.3 Some Important Facts About Common Food

Bell peppers, Green tea: It's loaded with antioxidants
Papaya : Papain is a strong digestive aid.
Broccoli: It is high in many nutrients, including fiber, vitamin C, vitamin K, iron, and potassium.
Strawberries: loaded with vitamin C and powerful antioxidants.
Pineapple: Bromelain is a type of enzyme called a proteolytic enzyme. It is found in pineapple juice and in the pineapple stem. Bromelain causes the body to make substances that fight pain and swelling. Bromelain also contains chemicals that seem to interfere with tumor cells and slow blood clotting.
Oranges: The vitamin C found in oranges.
Kiwi. Kiwis are high in Vitamin C and dietary fiber.

Foods rich in copper include sesame seeds, cashews, pumpkin seeds, beet greens, spinach, kale, and beans(Vitamin C and copper are two nutrients required to covert dopamine to norepinephrine).

Bananas: Bananas are a healthy source of fiber, potassium, vitamin B6, vitamin C, and various antioxidants and phytonutrients.

Chocolate: good mix of minerals ,norepinephrine(norepinephrine, which contribute to arousal and activation)

Almond: Almonds contain lots of healthy fats, fiber, protein, magnesium and vitamin E.

Apple: fiber-rich food.

Okra or lady finger: rich in vitamins A and C

Bitter gourd: As a rich source of antioxidants, flavonoids, and other polyphenol compounds, bitter gourd may help to reduce your risks for a number of health issues.

Lemon: Lemons contain 77 mg of vitamin C per 100 grams, with one medium lemon delivering 92% of the DV.

Walnut: Walnuts are rich in heart-healthy fats and high in antioxidants

Carrot: Carrots are excellent sources of nutrients like potassium, antioxidants, and vitamin A, among many others. Beta - carotene, a type of carotenoid, is the nutrient that turns carrots orange and also promotes good health.

Brazil nut: Brazil nuts are the richest source of selenium,

Pistachio pistachios are one of the most vitamin B6-

rich foods around.

Tofu: Tofu contains several anti-inflammatory, anti-oxidant phyto-chemicals

Sources of calcium include:

milk, cheese and other dairy foods, green leafy vegetables – such as curly kale, okra and spinach etc.Phosphorous food source Yogurt, milk, lentil, potatoes etc and Oxygen only from tree and plant.

8.4 Pineal Gland

The pineal gland is a small, pea-shaped gland in the brain. Its function isn't fully understood. Researchers do know that it produces and regulates some hormones, including melatonin.

Melatonin is best known for the role it plays in regulating sleep patterns. Sleep patterns are also called circadian rhythms.The pineal gland is a tiny organ in the centre of the brain that played an important role in Descartes 'philosophy. He regarded it as the principal seat of the soul and the place in which all our thoughts are formed. In this entry, we discuss Descartes 'views concerning the pineal gland. We also put them into a historical context by describing the main theories about the functions of the pineal gland that were proposed before and after his time.Towards the end of the nineteenth century, Madame Blavatsky, the founder of theosophy, identified the "third eye" discovered by the comparative anatomists of her time with the "eye of Shiva" of "the Hindu mystics" and concluded that the pineal body of modern man is an atrophied vestige of this "organ of spiritual vision" (Blavatsky 1888, vol. 2, pp. 289–306). This theory is still fairly well-known today.Once called the 'third eye, 'the pineal gland is a small gland located deep in the center of the brain. Named for its pinecone shape, this gland secretes melatonin, which plays a role in the body's internal clock. The pineal gland was one of the last brain organs to be discovered and has been the subject of much mythology and speculation. The seventeenth-century French philosopher Rene Descartes thought the soul was located in the pineal gland.

The pineal gland is key to the body's internal clock because it regulates the body's circadian rhythms. Circadian rhythms are the daily rhythms of the body, including signals that make someone feel tired, sleep, wake up, and feel alert around the same time each day. The pineal gland secretes melatonin, which is a hormone that helps regulate circadian rhythms. Melatonin is produced according to the amount of light a person is exposed to.

The pineal gland releases greater amounts of melatonin when it is dark, which points to melatonin's role in sleep. Many supplement manufacturers offer melatonin as a "natural" sleep aid.The pituitary gland is a gland that protrudes from a part of the brain called the hypothalamus. The hypothalamus is linked to a wide range of hormonal functions, including growth and thyroid function. Older research suggests that the pineal gland can alter the behavior of the pituitary gland.

Melatonin may block the pituitary gland from secreting hormones that play essential roles in the development of the ovaries and testes and regulate

Notably high melatonin concentrations have been measured in popular beverages such as coffee, tea, wine, and beer, and crops including corn, rice, wheat, barley, and oats.In some common foods and beverages, including coffee and walnuts,the concentration of melatonin has been estimated or measured to be sufficiently high to raise the blood level of melatonin above daytime baseline values.

Naturally-occurring melatonin has been reported in foods including tart cherries, bananas and grapes, rice and cereals, herbs, plums, olive oil, wine and beer. When birds ingest melatonin-rich plant feed, such as rice, the melatonin binds to melatonin receptors in their brains.When humans consume foods rich in melatonin, such as banana, pineapple, and orange, the blood levels of melatonin increase significantly.

corns,rice,nonglutinous black rice,wheat, barley and oats,Grapes , cherries and strawberries,Tomatoes and peppers ,Mushrooms,white and black mustard seeds,pistachio,beer and wine,coffee beans,linseed ,olive oil etc.Since the secretion of endogenous melatonin decreases after childhood, increasing dietary consumption could be a good option. The studies showed that intake of the food rich in melatonin may gain health impacts by increasing circulating melatonin .Melatonin has been identified and qualified in a large number of foods. The content of melatonin is higher in eggs and fish than that in meat in animal foods, while in plant foods, the highest contents of melatonin was found in nuts, and some cereals and germinated legumes or seeds are also rich in melatonin. Mushrooms are also good dietary sources of melatonin.

8.3 Others Technique For Depression Reduction

- Deep breathing
- Meditation
- Exercise (non-high intensity, gentle walking, swimming, yoga, weight lifting)
- Take a technology detox (to take a break from using electronic devices or certain media for a period of time)
- Acupuncture or Acupressure
- Spend time with pets, family or friends who bring you joy
- Listen to or watch comedy
- Time in Nature
- Soothing Music
- Practice positive thinking
- Gratitude journal
- Reading
- Exercise
- Sunbath

9.HISTORY AND NOVEL, POEMS

"Absent of light is called darkness similar way absent of knowledge is called conscienceless. Happiness with conscience is more meaningful to find our destiny than happiness in darkness with maze."

The psychological and philosophical pursuit of happiness began in China, India and Greece nearly 2,500 years ago with Confucius, Buddha, Socrates, and Aristotle.

(https://www.pursuit-of-happiness.org/history-of-happiness/)

Buddha:

For Buddha, the path to happiness starts from an understanding of the root causes of suffering. Those who consider Buddha a pessimist because of his concern with suffering have missed the point. In fact, he is a skillful doctor — he may break the bad news of our suffering, but he also prescribes a proactive course of treatment. In this metaphor, the medicine is the Buddha's teachings of wisdom and compassion known as *Dharma*, and the nurses that encourage us and show us how to take the medicine are the Buddhist community or *Sangha*. The illness however, can only be cured if the patient follows the doctor's advice and follows the course of treatment — the Eightfold Path, the core of which involves control of the mind.

In Buddhism, this treatment is not a simple medicine to be swallowed, but a daily practice of mindful thought and action that we ourselves can test scientifically through our own experience. Meditation is, of course, the most well known tool of this practice, but contrary to popular belief, it is not about detaching from the world. Rather it is a tool to train the mind not to dwell in the past or the future, but to live in the here and now, the realm in which we can experience peace most readily. These Four Noble Truths, monks, are actual, unerring, not otherwise. Therefore, they are called noble truths. (Samyutta Nikaya 56.27)

1. Life is means Dukkha (mental dysfunction or suffering).
2. Dukkha arises from craving.

3. Dukkha can be eliminated.

4. The way to the elimination of dukkha is the Eightfold Path.

Buddha believed that dukkha ultimately arose from ignorance and false knowledge. While dukkha is usually defined as suffering, "mental dysfunction" is closer to the original meaning. In a similar vein, Huston Smith explains dukkha by using the metaphor of a shopping cart that we "try to steer from the wrong end" or bones that have gone "out of joint" (Smith, 1991, p. 101). Because of such a mental misalignment, all movement, thoughts and creation that flow out can never be wholly satisfactory. In short, we can never be completely happy.

The Eightfold Path:The eightfold path is often divided into the three categories

of wisdom (right view/understanding,right intention),

ethical conduct (right speech, right action, right livelihood)

mental cultivation (right effort, right mindfulness, right concentration).

The Eightfold Path is a practical and systematic way out of ignorance, eliminating dukkha from our minds and our lifestyle through mindful thoughts and actions. It is presented as a whole system, but the three paths associated with the area of mental cultivation are particularly relevant to the happiness that we can find in equanimity, or peace of mind.

Equanimity: Peace of Mind & Happiness

If by leaving a small pleasure one sees a great pleasure, let a wise person leave the small pleasure and look to the great. (Dhammapada 290 / Müller & Maguire, 2002.)

Buddhism pursues happiness by using knowledge and practice to achieve mental equanimity. In Buddhism, equanimity, or peace of mind, is achieved by detaching oneself from the cycle of craving that produces dukkha. So by achieving a mental state where you can detach from all the passions, needs and wants of life, you free yourself and achieve a state of transcendent bliss and well-being.

As described in the first verse of the Dhammapada, for Buddha, mental dysfunction begins in the mind. The Buddha encouraged his followers to pursue "tranquility" and "insight" as the mental qualities that would lead to Nirvana, the Ultimate Reality. As mentioned earlier, the Eightfold Path as a whole is said to help one achieve these qualities. In particular, the areas of mental cultivation, which include right effort, right mindfulness and right concentration, are the mental skills and tools used for achieving happiness.

Buddha: Right Effort

The Buddha once described the mind as a wild horse. In the Eightfold Path, he recommends practicing "right effort" by first avoiding and then clearing our minds of negative, unwholesome thoughts. Once that is achieved, one perfects a wholesome, tranquil state of mind through the practice of positive thinking. This ongoing effort promotes a state of mind that is conducive to the practice of mindfulness and concentration (meditation).

Mindfulness

Mindfulness is one of the most influential teachings of Buddhism and has filtered into popular culture as well as modern psychotherapy. The Buddha felt that it was imperative to cultivate right mindfulness for all aspects of life in order to see things as they really are, or in other words, to "stop and smell the roses." He encouraged keen attention and awareness of all things through the four foundations of mindfulness:

1. Contemplation of the body

2. Contemplation of feelings

3. Contemplation of states of mind

4. Contemplation of phenomena

In a word, mindfulness is about experiencing the moment with an attitude of openness and freshness to all and every experience. Through right mindfulness, one can free oneself from passions and cravings, which so often make us prisoners of past regrets or future preoccupations.

Right Concentration and Meditation

A monk who with tranquil mind has chosen to live in a bare cell knows an unearthly delight in gaining a clearer and clearer perception of the true law.

(Dhammapada 373 / Müller & Maguire, 2002.)

Right Concentration is a mental discipline that aims to transform your mind. As the core practice of "meditation," right concentration is a foundational activity within Buddhist thought and practice.

ACCORDING TO BUDDHA, THERE ARE FOUR STAGES OF DEEPER CONCENTRATION CALLED DHYANA:

1. The first stage of concentration is one in which mental hindrances and impure intentions disappear and a sense of bliss is achieved.

2. In the second stage, activities of the mind come to an end and only bliss remains.

3. In the third stage, bliss itself begins to disappear.

4. In the final stage, all sensations including bliss disappear and are replaced by a total peace of mind, which Buddha described as a deeper sense of happiness.

Compassion
The disciples of Gautama are always well awake, and their minds day and night always delight in compassion.

(Dhammapada 300 / Müller & Maguire, 2002.)

Stories of Buddha's compassion and consideration for all life abound. He taught truth and he also taught compassion because he saw personal happiness as related to the happiness of others, humans and otherwise. Such a lesson is reflected in both the way he lived and the way he died. In life, it was said that the Buddha forewent Nirvana in order to teach others the keys to transcendence. In death, the story goes that a follower accidentally poisoned Buddha. As he was dying, he comforted this follower by assuring him that the meal he had just eaten was one of his two most blessed meals: the first meal was the one he had to break his fast under the bodhi tree, and this second meal of rotten mushrooms was the meal that would bring him to Nirvana.

Conclusion

The journey to attain a deeper form of happiness requires an unflinching look into the face of a reality where all life is seen as dukkha or mental dysfunction. Buddhism is a philosophy and practice that is extremely concerned with the mind and its various delusions, misunderstandings and cravings but, happily for us, sees a way out through higher consciousness and mindful practice.

Perhaps it is because of this seemingly dim view of reality that happiness in Buddhism is so tremendously full; the ideas contained in Buddha's teachings point to a thorough engagement with lived reality. Ironically, it is through such an engagement with one's self, the world and reality that one is able to achieve a transcendent happiness. Equanimity, a deep sense of well-being and happiness, is attainable through proper knowledge and practice in everyday life. (https://www.pursuit-of-happiness.org/history-of-happiness/buddha/)

Socrates

Socrates(https://www.pursuit-of-happiness.org/history-of-happiness/socrates/): Socrates lived in Athens Greece his entire life (469-399 BC), cajoling his fellow citizens to think hard about questions of truth and justice, convinced as he was that "the unexamined life is not worth living." While claiming that his wisdom consisted merely in "knowing that he knew nothing," Socrates did have certain beliefs, chief among them that happiness is obtainable by human effort. Specifically, he recommended gaining rational control over your desires and harmonizing the different parts of your soul. Doing so would produce a divine-like state of inner tranquility that the external would could not effect. True to his word, he cheerfully faced his own death, discussing philosophy right up to the moments before he took the lethal hemlock. Through his influence on Plato and Aristotle, a new era of philosophy was inaugurated and the course of western civilization was decisively shaped.

Socrates – A Little Background

A Case Study of a Happy Person

The Roman philosopher Cicero once said that Socrates "wrested philosophy from the heavens and brought it down to earth." Prior to Socrates, Greek philosophy consisted primarily of metaphysical questions: why does the world stay up? Is the world composed of one substance or many substances? But living amidst the horrors of the Peloponnesian War, Socrates was more interested in ethical and social issues: what is the best way to live? Why be moral when immoral people seem to benefit more? Is happiness satisfying one's desires or is it virtuous activity?

Famously Socrates was more adept at asking such questions than spoon-feeding us the answers. His "Socratic method" consisted of a process of questioning designed to expose ignorance and clear the way for knowledge. Socrates himself admits that he is ignorant, and yet he became the wisest of all men through this self-knowledge. Like an empty cup Socrates is open to receive the waters of knowledge wherever he may find them; yet through his cross examinations he finds only people who claim to be wise but really know nothing. Most of our cups are too filled with pride, conceit, and beliefs we cling to in order to give us a sense of identity and security. Socrates represents the challenge to all our preconceived opinions, most of which are based on hearsay and faulty logic. Needless to say, many people resented Socrates when he pointed this out to them in the agon or public square.

The price Socrates paid for his honest search for truth was death: he was convicted of "corrupting the youth" and sentenced to die by way of Hemlock poisoning. But here we see the life of Socrates testifies to the truth of his teachings. Instead of bemoaning his fate or blaming the gods, Socrates faces his death with equanimity, even cheerfully discussing philosophy with his friends in the moments before he takes the lethal cup. As someone who trusted in the eternal value of the soul, he was unafraid to meet death, for he believed it was the ultimate release of the soul from the limitations of the body. In contrast to the prevailing Greek belief that death is being condemned to Hades, a place of punishment or wandering aimless ghost-like existence, Socrates looks forward to a place where he can continue his questionings and gain more knowledge. As long as there is a mind that earnestly seeks to explore and understand the world, there will be opportunities to expand one's consciousness and achieve an increasingly happier mental state.

Socrates Three Dialogues on Happiness: The Euthydemus, The Symposium, and The Republic
Although Socrates didn't write anything himself, his student Plato wrote a voluminous number of dialogues with him as the central character. Scholarly debate still rages as to the relationship between Socrates' original teachings and Plato's own evolving ideas. In what follows, we will treat the views expressed by Socrates the character as Socrates' own views, though it should be noted that the closer we get to a "final answer" or comprehensive theory of happiness, the closer we are to Plato than to the historical Socrates.

The Euthydemus
This is the first piece of philosophy in the West to discuss the concept of happiness, but it is not merely of historical interest. Rather, Socrates presents an argument as to what happiness is that is as powerful today

as when he first discussed it over 2400 years ago. Basically, Socrates is concerned to establish two main points: 1) happiness is what all people desire: since it is always the end (goal) of our activities, it is an unconditional good, 2) happiness does not depend on external things, but rather on how those things are used. A wise person will use money in the right way in order to make his life better; an ignorant person will be wasteful and use money poorly, ending up even worse than before. Hence we cannot say that money by itself will make one happy. Money is a conditional good, only good when it is in the hands of a wise person. This same argument can be redeployed for any external good: any possessions, any qualities, even good looks or abilities. A handsome person, for example, can become vain and manipulative and hence misuse his physical gifts. Similarly, an intelligent person can be an even worse criminal than an unintelligent one.

Socrates then presents the following stunning conclusion:

"So what follows from what we've said? Isn't it this, that of the other things none is either good or bad, and that of these two, wisdom is good and ignorance bad?"

He agreed.

"Well then let's have a look at what's left," I said. "Since all of us desire to be happy, and since we evidently become so on account of our use—that is our good use— of other things, and since knowledge is what provides this goodness of use and also good fortune, every man must, as seems plausible, prepare himself by every means for this: to be as wise as possible. Right?"

'Yes," he said. (281e2-282a7)

Here Socrates makes it clear that the key to happiness is not to be found in the goods that one accumulates, or even the projects that form the ingredients of one's life, but rather in the agency of the person himself who gives her life a direction and focus. Also clear from this is a repudiation of the idea that happiness consists merely in the satisfaction of our desires. For in order to determine which desires are worth satisfying, we have to apply our critical and reflective intelligence (this is what Socrates calls "wisdom"). We have to arrive at an understanding of human nature and discover what brings out the best in the human being–which desires are mutually reinforcing, and which prevent us from achieving a sense of overall purpose and well-functioning. No doubt we can also conclude from this that Socrates was the first "positive psychologist," insofar as he called for a scientific understanding of the human mind in order to find out what truly leads to human happiness.

The Symposium
This dialogue takes place at a dinner party, and the topic of happiness is raised when each of the partygoers takes a turn to deliver a speech in honor of Eros, the god of love and desire. The doctor Eryximachus claims that this god above all others is capable of bringing us happiness, and the playwright Aristoph-

anes agrees, claiming that Eros is "that helper of mankind...who eliminates those evils whose cure brings the greatest happiness to the human race." (186b) For Eryximachus, Eros is that force which gives life to all things, including human desire, and thus is the source of all goodness. For Aristophanes, Eros is the force which seeks to reunite the human being after its split into male and female opposites.

For Socrates, however, Eros has a darker side, since as the representation of desire, he is constantly longing and never completely satisfied. As such he cannot be a full god, since divinity is supposed to be eternal and self-sufficient. Nevertheless, Eros is vitally important in the human quest for happiness, since he is the intermediary between the human and the divine. Eros is that power of desire which begins by seeking physical pleasures, but can be retrained to pursue the higher things of the mind. The human being can be educated to move away from the love of beautiful things which perish to the pure love of Beauty itself. When this happens, the soul finds complete satisfaction. Socrates describes this as a kind of rapture or epiphany, when the scales falls from one's eyes and one beholds the truth of one's existence. As he says:

If...man's life is ever worth the living, it is when he has attained this vision of the soul of beauty. And once you have seen it, you will never be seduced again by the charm of gold, of dress, of comely boys, you will care nothing for the beauties that used to take your breath away...and when one discerns this beauty one will perceive the true virtue, not virtue's semblance. And when a man has brought forth and reared this perfect virtue, he shall be called the friend of god, and if ever it is capable of man to enjoy immortality, it shall then be given to him. (212d)

While Socrates and Plato seemed to believe that this mystic rapture was primarily to be achieved by philosophy, there will be others who take up this theme but give it either a religious or aesthetic interpretation: Christian thinkers will pronounce that the greatest happiness is the pure vision of God (Thomas Aquinas), while others will proclaim that it is a vision of beauty in music or art (Schopenhauer). In any case, the idea is that this one overwhelming experience of truth, beauty or the divine, will make all the sufferings and tribulations of our lives meaningful and worth experiencing. It is the Holy Grail that comes only after all our adventures in the wild.

The Republic

In Plato's masterpiece The Republic, Socrates wants to prove that the just person is happier than the unjust person. Since, as he already argued in the Euthydemus, all men naturally desire happiness, then we should all seek to live a just life. In the process of making this argument, Socrates makes many other points regarding a) what happiness is, b) the relationship between pleasure and happiness, and c) the relationship between pleasure, happiness, and virtue (morality).

The first argument Socrates presents concerns the

analogy between health in the body and justice in the soul. We all certainly prefer to be healthy than unhealthy, but health is nothing but the harmony among different parts of the body, each carrying out its proper function. Justice, it turns out, is a similar kind of harmony, but among the different parts of the soul. Injustice on the other hand is defined as a "sort of civil war" between the parts of the soul (444a): a rebellion in which one rogue element—the desirous part of our natures—usurps reason as the controlling power. In contrast, the just soul is one that possesses "psychic harmony:" no matter what life throws at the just man, he never loses his inner composure, and can maintain peace and tranquility despite the harshest of life's circumstances. Here Socrates effectively redefines the conventional concept of happiness: it is defined in terms of internal benefits and characteristics rather than external ones.

The second argument concerns an analysis of pleasure. Socrates wants to show that living a virtuous life brings greater pleasure than living an unvirtuous life. The point is already connected with the previous one, insofar as one could argue that the psychic harmony that results from a just life brings with it greater peace and inner tranquility, which is more pleasant than the unjust life which tends to bring inner discord, guilt, stress, anxiety, and other characteristics of an unhealthy mind. But Socrates wants to show that there are further considerations to emphasize the higher pleasures of the just life: not merely peace of mind, but the excitement of pursuing knowledge, produces an almost godlike state in the human being. The philosopher is at the pinnacle of this pursuit: having cast off the blinders of ignorance, he can now explore the higher realm of truth, and this experience makes every merely physical pleasure pale in comparison.

Perhaps the most powerful argument, and the one Socrates actually 'dedicates to Zeus' (583b-588a) can be called the "relativity of pleasure" argument. Most pleasures are not really pleasures at all, but merely result from the absence of pain. For example, if I am very sick and suddenly get better, I might call my new state pleasurable, but only because it is a relief from my sickness. Soon enough this pleasure will become neutral as I adjust to my new condition. Nearly all of our pleasures are relative like this, hence they are not purely pleasurable. Another example would be the experience of getting high on drugs: this can produce a high state of pleasure in the short-term, but then will inevitably lead to the opposite state of pain. Socrates' claim is however that there are some pleasures that are not relative, because they concern higher parts of the soul that are not bound to the relativity produced by physical things. These are the philosophical pleasures—the pure pleasure of coming to a greater understanding of reality.

A few hundred years after Socrates, the philosopher Epicurus would take up Socrates' argument and make a very interesting distinction between "positive" and "negative" pleasures. Positive pleasure depends on pain because it is nothing but the removal of pain: you are thirsty so you drink a glass of water to get some relief. Negative pleasure, however, is that state of harmony where you no longer feel any pain and hence no longer need a positive pleasure to get rid of the pain. Positive pleasure is always quantifiable and falls on a scale: do you have more or less pleasure from sex rather than from eating, for example. Positive pleasures are bound to be frustrating as a result, since there will always be a contrast between the state you are in now and a "higher" state which would make your present experience appear less desirable. Negative pleasures, however, are not quantifiable: you cannot ask "how much are you not feeling hungry?" Epicurus concludes from this that the true state of happiness is the state of negative pleasure, which is basically the state of not experiencing any unfulfilled desires. Needless to say, one can also make connections between this perspective and the Buddhist concept of achieving nirvana through the removal of desire, or the modern writer Eckhart Tolle's injunction to experience the simple stillness of being without the interference of positive thoughts and emotions.

Conclusion

Socrates (as seen through the lens of Plato) can be said to espouse the following ideas about happiness:

All human beings naturally desire happiness
Happiness is obtainable and teachable through human effort
Happiness is directive rather than additive: it depends

not on external goods, but how we use these external goods (whether wisely or unwisely)

Happiness depends on the "education of desire" whereby the soul learns how to harmonize its desires, redirecting its gaze away from physical pleasures to the love of knowledge and virtue

Virtue and Happiness are inextricably linked, such that it would be impossible to have one without the other.

The pleasures that result from pursuing virtue and knowledge are of a higher quality than the pleasures resulting from satisfying mere animal desires. Pleasure is not the goal of existence, however, but rather an integral aspect of the exercise of virtue in a fully human life.

(https://www.pursuit-of-happiness.org/history-of-happiness/socrates/)

Aristotle

(https://www.pursuit-of-happiness.org/history-of-happiness/aristotle/)

Aristotle is one of the greatest thinkers in the history of western science and philosophy, making contributions to logic, metaphysics, mathematics, physics, biology, botany, ethics, politics, agriculture, medicine, dance and theatre. He was a student of Plato who in turn studied under Socrates. Although we do not actually possess any of Aristotle's own writings intended for publication, we have volumes of the lecture notes he delivered for his students; through these Aristotle was to exercise his profound influence through the ages. Indeed, the medieval outlook is sometimes considered to be the "Aristotelian worldview" and St. Thomas Aquinas simply refers to Aristotle as "The Philosopher" as though there were no other.

Aristotle was the first to classify areas of human knowledge into distinct disciplines such as mathematics, biology, and ethics. Some of these classifications are still used today, such as the species-genus system taught in biology classes. He was the first to devise a formal system for reasoning, whereby the validity of an argument is determined by its structure rather than its content. Consider the following syllogism: All men are mortal; Socrates is a man; therefore, Socrates is mortal. Here we can see that as long as the premises are true, the conclusion must also be true, no matter what we substitute for "men or "is mortal." Aristotle's brand of logic dominated this area of thought until the rise of modern symbolic logic in the late 19th Century.

Aristotle was the founder of the Lyceum, the first scientific institute, based in Athens, Greece. Along with his teacher Plato, he was one of the strongest advocates of a liberal arts education, which stresses the education of the whole person, including one's moral character, rather than merely learning a set of skills. According to Aristotle, this view of education is necessary if we are to produce a society of happy as well as productive individuals.

...the function of man is to live a certain kind of life,

and this activity implies a rational principle, and the function of a good man is the good and noble performance of these, and if any action is well performed it is performed in accord with the appropriate excellence: if this is the case, then happiness turns out to be an activity of the soul in accordance with virtue. (Nicomachean Ethics, 1098a13)

He is happy who lives in accordance with complete virtue and is sufficiently equipped with external goods, not for some chance period but throughout a complete life. (Nicomachean Ethics, 1101a10)

according to Aristotle, what is happiness?

Happiness is the ultimate end and purpose of human existence

Happiness is not pleasure, nor is it virtue. It is the exercise of virtue.

Happiness cannot be achieved until the end of one's life. Hence it is a goal and not a temporary state.

Happiness is the perfection of human nature. Since man is a rational animal, human happiness depends on the exercise of his reason.

Happiness depends on acquiring a moral character, where one displays the virtues of courage, generosity, justice, friendship, and citizenship in one's life. These virtues involve striking a balance or "mean" between an excess and a deficiency.

Happiness requires intellectual contemplation, for this is the ultimate realization of our rational capacities.

(https://www.pursuit-of-happiness.org/history-of-happiness/aristotle/)

Famous Book/Works On Happiness:

Counter Clockwise. Dr. Langer ;
Love 2.0: Finding Happiness and Health in Moments of Connection Book by Barbara Fredrickson; Happiness: Unlocking the Mysteries of Psychological Wealth by Ed Diener;
The Summa Theologica by Thomas Aquinas; The Zhuangzi(Zhuangzi. (1968). The Complete Works of Chuang Tzu (B. Watson, Trans.). New York: Columbia University Press.); Maslow, A.H. (1980). *The Farther Reaches of Human Nature (An Esalen Book)*. New York, NY: Penguin.

Some poems on life may read :

9.1 Death

Death is true,
Death is real,
Death is destiny,
Death is inevitable,
Death is unavoidable.
But suicide is sin,
Suicide is avoidable.
Suicide is evitable.

9.2 Remember

Joy Harjo - 1951-

Remember the sky that you were born under,
know each of the star's stories.

Remember the moon, know who she is.
Remember the sun's birth at dawn, that is the
strongest point of time. Remember sundown
and the giving away to night.
Remember your birth, how your mother struggled
to give you form and breath. You are evidence of
her life, and her mother's, and hers.
Remember your father. He is your life, also.
Remember the earth whose skin you are:
red earth, black earth, yellow earth, white earth
brown earth, we are earth.
Remember the plants, trees, animal life who all have their
tribes, their families, their histories, too. Talk to them,
listen to them. They are alive poems.
Remember the wind. Remember her voice. She knows the
origin of this universe.
Remember you are all people and all people are you.
Remember you are this universe and this universe is you.
Remember all is in motion, is growing, is you.
Remember language comes from this.
Remember the dance language is, that life is.

Remember.

9.3 Interrogation Of The Hanged Man

Monica Youn

> What is your face?
> > A house, of sorts.
>
> What is your foot?
> > A chipped stone blade.
>
> What did you dream?
> > A rain-washed road.
>
> What did it mean?
> > It meant nothing.
>
> What have you learned?
> > The sky forgives.
>
> What does it forgive?
> > Each jet its wake.
>
> What do you want?
> > A smile, of sorts.
>
> No, what do you want?
> > I want nothing.
>
> What's in your hand?
> > A leafless twig.
>
> No. Show me. What's that in your hand?

"life with smile is more important than any other things but not a cost of others."

9.4. Why Am I

Why am I smile,
Why am I happy,
Why am I jolly,
Why am I glee,

KAMAL KUMAR PRAJAPAT

Why am I exultant,
Why am I delighted,
Why am I glad,
'cause life is mine.

10. LOGIC & SCIENCE

"Science is the body and Mathematics is the soul, when both resonant and communicate with each other than its byproduct is happiness."

Perception means one's statement is right but other's also and fights to each others as both are right. Faith is religious belief of human and it's very common and cannot be declined. It cannot be separated from human life. The mixing of faith and perception gives wrong idea and we are far away from reality. Science and logic are the only ways which give you a path in darkness.Anything difficult good for for brain and health.

10.1 Death

(International Guidelines for the Determination of Death – Phase I May 30-31, 2012 Montreal Forum Report WHO):

Human death was defined based on measurable biomedical standards. Participants supported a movement away from anatomically-based terms such as brain death or cardiac death that erroneously imply the death of that organ. Emphasis was placed on the cessation of neurological or circulatory function and the predominance of brain function for determination of death.

"Death occurs when there is permanent loss of capacity for consciousness and loss of all brain-stem functions. This may result from permanent cessation of circulation and/or after catastrophic brain injury. In the context of death determination, 'permanent' refers to loss of function that cannot resume spontaneously and will not be restored through intervention."

This definition is based on the cessation of function (the primary and fundamental purpose of an organ that can be assessed by observation and examination and is necessary for sustained life) rather than activities (physiologic properties of cells and groups of cells that can be measured by laboratory means).

From The Gita : Chapter 2.27

जातस्य हि ध्रुवो मृत्युर्ध्रुवं जन्म मृतस्य च |
तस्मादपरिहार्येऽर्थे न त्वं शोचितुमर्हसि || 27||

jātasya hi dhruvo mrityur dhruvam janma mritasya cha

tasmād aparihārye 'rthe na tvam śhochitum arhasi

meaning difficult words :

jātasya—for one who has been born; hi—for; dhruvaḥ —certain; mrityuḥ—death; dhruvam—certain; janma —birth; mritasya—for the dead; cha—and; tasmāt— therefore; aparihārye arthe—in this inevitable situation; na—not; tvam—you; śhochitum—lament; arhasi—befitting

Death is certain for one who has been born, and re-birth is inevitable for one who has died. Therefore, you should not lament over the inevitable.

From The Quran (https://en.wikipedia.org/wiki/Islamic_view_of_death#:~:text=Probably%20the%20most%2Dfrequently%20quoted,the%20sight%20of%20Allah%20is): The Quran at its several places discusses the issue of death. Death is inevitable. No matter how much people try to escape death, it will reach everyone (Q50:19). Again, those who deny resurrection and afterlife, and thus challenge God, the Quran challenges them by saying that why these people then do not put back the soul which has reached the throat (of the dying person) and is about to escape the body? (56:83–84). It also says that when death approaches the sinners and disbelievers, and they sense the upcoming chastisement, they pray to God to go back to life to do some good deeds; but this will never be granted (23:99–100). Probably the most-frequently quoted verse of the Quran about death is: "Every soul shall taste death, and only on the Day of Judgment will you be paid your full recompense." At another place, the Quran urges mankind: "And die not except in a state of Islam" (3:102) because "Truly, the religion in the sight of Allah is Islam" (3:19). Other verses related with this issue are: "He (Allah) who created death and life, so that He may test you as to which of you is better in deeds. And He is the All-Mighty, the Most-Forgiving" (67:2); "Certainly, they see it (resurrection) as distant, but We see it as near" (70:6–7).

Death is nothing but absence of soul in body. Human body is called a living human only if he has soul and body parts hearts, brain working. One who born certainly will die. Soul value for male or woman are equal, it just transfers to one body to other not necessary human. Total soul on universe is constant only transform from one form another.

Death has no time and date but many of them can feel they are going to be died. Everyone has his destiny so don't warry about others.

When we born the countdown of death start from that day nothing matters what's the age. The probability of death is equal to all and it is fifty-fifty compared to other in natural conditions. When any one decide to die the probability of die increased than natural conditions.

No one can control the soul by any means ,who is less mental control may induce the soul effect but it is only mental disorder by induction of near environment.

10.2 Reincarnation

Reincarnation is possible in real. Soul always takes another body after dead but it is not necessary that that will be human. Soul can neither be controlled nor transfer by any human. It follows some undefined rule and his past act result. After birth, human gain environment knowledge and culture, acquire basic elements. There is no responsibility other's for his/her fault, he or herself fully responsible.soul always with you if you are truthful in voice.

10.3 Human Thinking And Power

1. All our ideas are compounded from a very small number of simple ideas, which form the alphabet of human thought.
2. Complex ideas proceed from simple ideas by a uniform and symmetrical combination, analogous to arithmetical multiplication.

suppose we say India has many state and population are more than 100 cr if combine then to fight other country, will loose battle as all combine infinity group has no power and in real negative.*So I ,only have identity and i am responsible for that and most powerful myself.* When i am adding every day nothing in my mind ,it becomes half mind.If i am adding every day every thing in my mind it becomes negative.

Belief and truth may give a solution of life but it shall be beneficial of humankind and others living things.If we have sadness and thinking continuous then depression increase exponentially.If person is lived longtime with sadness and dead after long time then his dead will be due to that sadness. If person rebirth then old birth unhappiness left in old birth so new birth always a new life without old unhappiness but may flashback old memory but no affect in new life. We shall believe in induction of behaviours if live in bad environment then would think/behave bad or vice versa but if provide a shield of thinking or behaviours this can be changed. In closed area (less interaction with out side) that have some static energy which is has no effect of behaviours and development internally but every static energy develop some effect which induce some type of energy which develop more internal energy more. In nutshell human being shall not be in closed space but have strong all internal energy from that closed space which induce more powerful outside energy and more success in life. Always we shall be internally strong only by experience of toughness of life.

Internal-energy and outside energy are co-related and synchronised with each other then real movement of life is going in forward direction and getting success as we want in life other wise filling depressed or bored or normal.

High spiritual(not related to God but feel like God affect)/internal Energy effect the other person and it may be filled by others.Black absorb all negative energy so feel black by closing eyes in day and think about the action or go to such place feel good so that negative feeling or negative energy may remove.

Human can feel negative Energy or feel other presence without seeing others.So we should open our sixth sence that is our mind wave beware of unwanted thinks.

Spiritual feeling may be one of or other thinks also but we should not dishonest with ourselves and be truthful always so our sixth sence can sence.

Human Mind has no limit ,it can move anywhere. Mind Energy wave has a power to move anywhere and stop the time and every physical thing become zero when this wave move in space.

10.4 Brain Induction And Resonance

When one person feels sleepiness, due to this, other person nearby all feel sleepiness similar way if we go in music party, after some time in party we also feel that we should dance. It is due to effect brain wave induction from one person to other. So, brain wave intensity increases by increasing no of person and it induces the effect to human thought. Happy environment creates happy environment, sad or depressed environment creates sad or depressed environment. Studies show that Binaural Beats or brain wave at specific frequency levels offer different experiences.

- Delta pattern/waves: Binaural beats in the delta pattern operate at a frequency of 0.5–4 Hz generate in deep sleep. Studies show that using this pattern can encourage deeper stages of sleep.
- Theta pattern(memory wave): Binaural Beats in the theta pattern operate at a frequency of 4--8 Hz ,generate in moderate sleep in kids /medidation in adult or in depression. Theta patterns improved relaxation, mood, and creativity.
- Alpha pattern/waves : Binaural Beats in the alpha pattern are at a frequency of 8–13 Hz ,generate in

wondering mind or day dream and have been shown to promote relaxation.

- Beta pattern/waves : Binaural Beats in the beta pattern are at a frequency of 13–30 Hz ,generate in attention state. This frequency improves concentration and alertness. However, it can also increase anxiety at the higher end of the range, so one needs to be mindful about using this kind of music.

- Gamma pattern/waves: This frequency pattern accounts for a range between 30–50 Hz. Studies show that these frequencies promote maintenance of arousal while a person is awake. So if you want to be alert and improve concentration, Gamma is where that's at.

Following link on YouTube may listen:

Delta waves : https://youtu.be/txQ6t4yPIM0

Theta waves :https://youtu.be/CreU9g302yU

Alpha waves : https://youtu.be/WPni755-Krg

Beta waves:https://youtu.be/HA6nSQawROM

Gamma wavs:https://youtu.be/9pJheICAck4

Electromagnetic Field, Radio Frequency And Microwave Radiation Affect On Health:

1.In the conclusion, in our small study the use of mobile phones for more than 90 min in a day is associated with increased problems of concentration and attention[1]

2.Earth magnetic field affect the human behaviour in uneven way for different-different time and intensity. every person feel differently in different affect by fol-

lowing outside condition :
1)time
2)weather
3)humidity
4)Earth ElectroMagnetic field
so if you feel bad then try or wait to change above conditions.

Dmt Visual:

DMT (N,N-Dimethyltryptamine) is a hallucinogenic tryptamine drug that occurs naturally in many plants and animals. It is also referred to as the "spirit molecule" due to the intense psychedelic experience.Although lesser known than other psychedelics such as LSD or magic mushrooms, DMT produces a brief but intense visual and auditory hallucinogenic experience.DMT is a white crystalline powder that is derived from certain plants found in Mexico, South America, and parts of Asia, such as *Psychotria viridis* and *Banisteriopsis caapi*.(https://www.medicalnewstoday.com/articles/306889)

YouTube link for DMT visual (Please read all instruction before watching)
https://youtu.be/Eso7f8MbWEg
Most Realistic DMT Trip Simulation Yet! (4K ULTRA HD) https://youtu.be/Zbx1O9172Ss
VIRTUAL DMT Powerful Hallucination Simulation https://youtu.be/UYn4i0pY4_k

10.5 Every False Statement Give One Fear

The most widely accepted definition of lying is the following: "A lie is a statement made by one who does not believe it with the intention that someone else shall be led to believe it" (Isenberg 1973, 248) (cf. "[lying is] making a statement believed to be false, with the intention of getting another to accept it as true" (Primoratz 1984, 54n2)). This definition does not specify the addressee, however. It may be restated as follows:

(L1)   To lie =to make a believed-false statement to another person with the intention that the other person believe that statement to be true.

L1 is the traditional definition of lying. According to L1, there are at least four necessary conditions for lying. First, lying requires that a person make a state-ment (statement condition). Second, lying requires that the person believe the statement to be false; that is, lying requires that the statement be untruthful (untruthfulness condition). Third, lying requires that the untruthful statement be made to another person (addressee condition). Fourth, lying requires that the person intend that that other person believe the un-truthful statement to be true (intention to deceive the addressee condition).
These four necessary conditions need to be explained before objections to L1 can be entertained and alter-native definitions can be considered.
"a successful or unsuccessful deliberate attempt, without

forewarning, to create in another a belief which the communicator considers to be untrue"
The first is that there is no deception unless the communicator intends to deceive. Untrue statements made by mistake are not deceptive, although they might cause a listener to be misled.Most people would agree that it is a virtue to accept responsibility for one's wrongdoing. We teach our children that it is better to admit to a wrongful act than to cover it up by lying.Nevertheless, the fact is that people often do fail to accept responsibility for their wrongful acts. Sometimes they do so by remaining silent. Other times they do so by falsely denying the accusations that are made against them or by engaging in acts of deception to avoid detection.

10.6 Pseudo-Positive Environment

Depression can be abated by creating pseudo environment by music, trip to liked place ,create artificial digital environment etc.

The exact future prediction of exact mind thinking and exact mood are impossible and no one can can predict exact time of thinking and mood .So be happy in present.
Our thinking or mind always affected by other most presence (in spite we want or not) so be careful about decisions and result also affected by others presence also.
We shall feel remorseful for all our sin, It is enough to feel sorry & reconcile with our odds.
Emotions are manipulated by prevarication many time for our profit that should not right for healthy re-

lation, It is good to be pristine in talking & behaviour.

10.7 Placebo Effect

It refers fake treatment of person .By seeing other, ourselves recover. It is confidence with other that that they are good and good repeat many times, other person feel good without any treatment. By saying good words or follow good habit of others, we can improve ourselves.

10.8 New Technology Effect On Human Happiness And Behaviour

New technology effect on human happiness and behavior:

New technology like social platform, video making application, update of life event in a movement and expression of feeling gives new satisfaction and we are going made about expressing ourself and status.IT companies using your emotion for their product or any other uses. Artificial Technology is analysing you emotion that what you need or will need, what is your balance, how you spend, what item get you trigger. Now your emotion on sells and it is easy to trap you for anything. We continuously using technology and use to for that. Our mind is not feeling easy without such aid, they are essential part of life presently.

In future your every life movement will be stored in database and by technology, companies will be able to find your thought process, your mood changing behaviour and will sell you your happiness to you. Your happiness will have some price depending the deep of happiness,

The app like Facebook, WhatsApp, google etc. that give a facility of new dimension of social behaviour and feel happy by using technology uses. So, technology knowledge is necessary before using the application or based on technology product.

10.9 Shake Your Head

This may reset your neurone.

11. EMOTION

"Emotions are nothing more than the thought of mind."

When baby born they have no emotion with present but as he develop and feel ,emotions come from inner side. As he grow take experience and practice other emotions.

Feelings develop different with age and experience new life feeling.

11.1 Forgiveness

To err is human, to forgive divine.

(इंसान ग़लतियों का पुतला है । क्षमा करने वाला भगवान के बराबर है।)

By Alexander Pope, Forgiveness can be a gift to yourself or to others, it may be something you receive, but it can also be a quality that describes a relationship where one must be capable of self-forgiveness in order to forgive others.

It loved to happen.

By Marcus Aurelius, If hope gives you wings, forgiveness will often be what you will need to get off the ground. As an aspect of resilience and a measure of psychological flexibility, forgiveness is best cultivated as an ongoing practice.One can become more forgiving, but as all positive solutions, it requires sustained effort and a significant investment of energy if we are to move in the direction of lasting change.

Forgiveness:It is status that is given to other that one's bad act are no more remember by other who give status.

Psychologists generally define forgiveness as a conscious, deliberate decision to release feelings of resentment or vengeance toward a person or group who has harmed you, regardless of whether they actually deserve your forgiveness.

 A person who has been done bad to other if that person feel guilty we shall give forgiveness, it is real calm.But in many cases bad person do not feel guilty and good person goes in deep depression.We should be control our emotions by different techniques mention in this book.

11.2 Jealous Anger Ego Negativity Emotions

How to deal with negative emotions
There are a number of coping strategies to deal with negative emotions. These include:
•   Don't blow things out of proportion by going over them time and again in your mind.
•   Try to be reasonable – accept that bad feelings are occasionally unavoidable and think of ways to make yourself feel better.
•   Relax – use pleasant activities like reading, walking or talking to a friend.
•   Learn – notice how grief, loss and anger make you feel, and which events trigger those feelings so you

can prepare in advance.

• Exercise – aerobic activity lowers your level of stress chemicals and allows you to cope better with negative emotions.

• Let go of the past – constantly going over negative events robs you of the present and makes you feel bad.
egative

11.3 Fight Or Flight' Response

Plutchik (1980) stated that there are eight basic emotions: joy, trust, fear, surprise, sadness, anticipation, anger and disgust. Plutchik went further by pairing the emotions with their opposites and then creating the wheel of emotions, which serves to elaborate on how complex and interactive our emotions are.

As mentioned, Plutchik paired the basic emotions with their polar opposites to help further develop his theory, so:

• Sadness is the opposite of Joy
• Anticipation is the opposite of Surprise

11.4 Emotion Wheel

• Anger is the opposite of Fear
• Disgust is the opposite of Trust

Plutchik's wheel is a strong visual representation of how our emotions present themselves. As you can see the core emotion decreases as you move outward on the wheel. Plutchik also used color to represent the intensity of the emotion: the darker the color, the more intense it is. So at its most intense trust becomes admiration, and at its least intense, acceptance.

It's a fantastic starting resource for helping us further develop our understanding of how our emotions present themselves, how they fluctuate and how they can interact with each other. It has informed further psychological research in this area and is often the foundation from which researchers exploring emotions have based their research (Eckman, 1999, Parrott, 2001, Lazarus & Lazarus, 1996).

Shaver et al (1987) and later Parrott (2001) proposed a 'tree' of emotions which broke emotions into primary, secondary and tertiary dimensions. This includes 6 primary emotions (love, joy, surprise, anger, sadness, and fear), with associated emotions that develop at the secondary level, and again at the tertiary level. For example, if the primary emotion is joy, the secondary emotions could include cheerfulness, optimism or enthrallments and the tertiary level could include pleasure, triumph or hope.

Cambria, Livingstone, and Hussain (2011) took Plutchik's wheel to another level and developed 'The Hourglass of Emotions'. In their book, they built on Plutchik's eight basic emotions and broke them down into four dimensions: sensitivity, attention, pleasantness, and aptitude. They also made distinctions between which of the emotions were positive (joy, trust, anger, and anticipation) or negative (disgust, sadness, fear, and surprise).

11.5 Negative Emotions

As we've begun to explore, negative emotions are

completely normal. Without them, we wouldn't be able to appreciate positive ones. At the same time, if you find you consistently have a tendency towards one particular emotion – especially a negative one – it's worth exploring why that might be.

 summarised eight of the more common negative emotions and why they might arise:

Anger

Anger is emotions start we are in mentally struggle.

Annoyance

Do you have a colleague who perhaps talks too loudly? Does your partner always leave their dirty dishes in the sink? Though we may like our colleague and love our partner these behaviours can make us feel really annoyed. Referring to Pluchik's wheel, it can see that annoyance is the weaker form of anger. While not as intense as anger, it's the result of a similar thought process – something has happened or someone is doing something you wish they wouldn't. And you have no control over it.

Fear

Fear is often cited as one of the core basic emotions, and that's because it's heavily linked with our sense of self-preservation. It's an evolved response to warn us about dangerous situations, unexpected obstacles or failures. We don't feel fear in order to feel distressed, on the contrary, it's there to help us navigate potential danger successfully. Embracing the emotion of fear and exploring why it arises can help you prepare yourself proactively to tackle challenges.

Anxiety

Much like fear, anxiety seeks to warn us about potential threats and dangers. It's often seen as a negative emotion as it's thought having an anxious disposition impairs judgment and our ability to act. New research has found the opposite.

Zein, Wyatt, and Grezes (2015) found having anxiety heightened participants ability to recognise faces with angry or fearful expressions. They measured electrical signals in the brain and found that non-clinically diagnosed participants shifted their energy from sensory (expressing the emotion) to motor (physical action) circuits. Basically, participants with anxiety were more ready to respond and react to perceived threats.

Sadness

When you miss a deadline, get a bad grade, or don't secure that job you had your hopes pinned on, you'll probably feel sad. Sadness happens when dissatisfied with ourselves, our achievements or the behavior of someone else around us. Sadness can be good to experience as it indicates to us that we passionate about something. It
can be a great catalyst to pursue change.

Guilt

Guilt is a complex emotion. We can feel this in relation to ourselves and past behaviours that we wish hadn't happened, but also in relation to how our behavior impacts those around us. Guilt is often referred to as a 'moral emotion '(Haidt, 2000) and can be another strong catalyst to encourage us to make changes in our life.

Apathy

Like guilt, apathy can be a complex emotion. If you've lost enthusiasm, motivation or interest in the things you've previously enjoyed, this could be related to apathy. Like anger, it can arise when we lose control over a scenario or situation but instead of becoming angry, we pursue a more passive-aggressive expression of rebellion.

Despair

Ever tried to achieve a certain task or goal multiple times and not succeeded? Did that make you feel like throwing your hands in the air, and camping out in bed with a large tub of ice cream for company? That's despair and it's an emotion that arises when we aren't getting the results we want. Despair gives us an excuse to give up on our desired goals and it comes back to a self-preservation tactic. Despair can actually be a useful reminder to take a break and restore, before continuing to pursue a challenging goal.

What Causes Negative Emotions and Why Do We Have Them?

In terms of causes, it could be a number of things for example:

- Anxiety felt around attending an interview for a new job
- Anger at being caught up in traffic

- Sadness at experiencing a break-up
- Annoyance that a colleague hasn't done the work for a big project
- Despair at not being able to stick to a new work-out regime

Emotions are a source of information (Schwarz and Clore, 1996) that help you understand what is going on around you. Negative emotions, in particular, can help you recognise threats (Zein, Wyatt and Grezes, 2015) and feel prepared to positively handle potential dangers (Biswas-Diener and Kashdan, 2014).

Above -ve emotions are shown on color line which is self explanatory.

Do We should take tension and Stop Negative Emotions Altogether?

We should not,

It's normal way for us to want to move away from emotions that make us feel sad. Negative emotions are normal and part of life. it's really important not to fall into the 'happiness trap' of believing that these emotions are a sign of weakness or low emotional intelligence. Trying to hide away from negative emotions, can lead to further emotional pain or loss.

As a human being, we are going through a full range of emotions in lifetime in response to rapidly changing situations and events. No emotion is without reason. It's when we begin to further explore and understand the purpose behind each emotion, that we learn new ways to respond which supports our emotional growth and sense of well-being.

When exploring negative emotions, it's also important to know that they are not the only source of information but also help to strike on negative events . Before act upon any emotion, seek to explore your previous experiences, knowledge and memories, personal values and desired outcomes. Emotions are a low-level reaction so you get to decide how you respond to them and not let them seize the behavior.

What are the Effects of Negative Emotions?
While understanding that negative emotions are a healthy part of life is important, there is a downside to giving them too much free reign.
If you spend too much time dwelling on negative emotions and the situations that might have caused them, you could go into a spiral of rumination. Rumination is the tendency to keep thinking, replaying, or obsessing over negative emotional situations and experiences (Nolen-Hoeksema, 1991). In this spiral of negative thinking, you can end up feeling worse and worse about the situation and yourself, the result of which could be a number of detrimental effects to your mental and physical wellbeing.
The problem with rumination is that it increases your brain's stress response circuit, meaning your body gets unnecessarily flooded with the stress hormone cortisol. There's considerable evidence that this is a driver for clinical depression (Izard, 2009).
Further research has linked the tendency to ruminate

to a number of harmful coping behaviours, such as overeating, smoking and alcohol consumption, alongside physical health consequences including insomnia, high blood pressure, cardiovascular disease, and clinical anxiety and depression (Gerin et al, 2012, Dimsdale, 2008, Everson et al, 1998).

Another study found that people who indulged in prolonged rumination after a negative emotional experience took longer to recover from the physiological impact of the experience (Szabo et al, 2017).

Rumination can be a difficult loophole to get out of, especially as most people don't realise they're stuck in ruminating rut and instead believe they are actively problem solving (Yapko, 2015). This can lead to further implications for mental and physical wellbeing.

Don't flog yourself for other faults.

Limbo condition can increase your tension many times just left such limbo condition & wait for some time.

Thinking about future gives a bleak idea, It may be for any age group think about what will do in future, what happens, are we safe many view come in mind.

Due to family ,earning resource like due to corona ,depression increased due to obscure future but think life is odyssey.

Due to corona many other problem developed like health issue financial issue ,mental issue affect the human.

The words "How are you",gives immense affect to other ,decrease negation fully.

Every think is not on your hand ,you can't control your or other life.

We believe in omen if we are to be going to start a new work.If something happen bad,we curse to omen & omen & feel satisfied,it is technique to put blame by logic to omen .In similar way bad act are justified or to be justified by blaming to such logic.

Life without onerous is dull,It has many ordeals in whole life & face by everyone in some of form.

Ostentatious manner or life style may give short pleasure but not a piece.

The technique of ostracise, give intense affect to mind of human so be careful from such technique & learn to live in any situation.

11.6 Human Safety Control System

our mind and body take input from safety information and negative emotions .safety with negative emotions feedback give safety enhance so our body try to work accordingly to balance that disturbance extra energy our another extra balance is required.

11.7 Déjà Vu

The sensation of having already experienced something that is occurring for the first time. Déjà vu is a French phrase that literally means "previously seen"
In present situation we feel or say something and suddenly we thought that this similar feeling or talking has been in past but we don't know ,when? We think that it may be dream.

The reason may be similar experience or dream in

past which may be due to dream become true or it may be due similar atmosphere events.

11.8 Contemplative Practice

When we think about the problem with quiet and serious for a sometime like 1hrs or 2 hrs or one day as think suitable, solution will come out of the problem. Problem thinking may involve many other thinks but by giving some more time problem may be solved. Always start from basic of the problem then move to complex thought. In many cases problems are complex but solutions are simple so thought for simple solution as possible.Other technique of Contemplative Practices are mindfulness, meditation, yoga, deep listening, contemplative reading and writing, and pilgrimage visit.(Read more at https://www.contemplativemind.org/practices/tree)

12.HEALTH AND WELL-BEING

"Always accept life challenge, they will shape you and your future. Just take a decision and go ahead with determination, It will right always."

12.1 How Can They Impact Our Health And Well-Being?

It's not negative emotions that directly impact our health and well-being, but how we react and process them when we do experience them that really counts. Staying stuck on negative emotions can increase our bodies' production of our stress hormone, cortisol, which in turn depletes our cognitive ability to problem solve proactively and can also damage our immune defences, making us more susceptible to other illness (Iliard, 2009). Chronic stress has also been linked to a shorter lifespan (Epel et al, 2004).Anger is the negative emotion that has been shown to have the biggest impact on our health and well-being, particularly where this is poorly managed. Studies have connected anger to various health concerns including high blood pressure, cardiovascular disease and digestive disorders (Hendricks et al, 2013).

Boerma (2007) linked unhealthy amounts of anger to increased levels of cortisol, which were implicated in decreased immune system efficiency. Boerma's research found that chronically angry people were more likely to have a cold, the flu, asthmatic symptoms and skin diseases such as rashes compared to non-chronically angry people.

Anger may effect our memory and sensory touch. emotions like anger when they are not handled in proactive ways.

12.2 Cost Benefit Analysis

we should analyse risk assessment and cost benefit. list all risk and cost with risk and action benefits. Analysis with ethical view and practical aspects and personal view with logical thoughts

12.3 Benefits Of Negative Emotions

It's not all doom and gloom. When handled well, negative emotions can have proven benefits for our well-being, and far more research has been poured into exploring this aspect of negative emotions.

I've summarised some of the key findings from the research for how negative emotions can benefit you:

1. Sadness Can Help You Pay More Attention To Detail

Where positive emotions signal that all is well in our immediate environment, negative emotions alert us that there are challenges or new stimuli that requires our more focused attention (Forgas, 2014). Sadness sends us the alert that something is no right and asks us to turn our attention to why this may be, what might be causing it, and what we need to do to fix it.

2. Anger Can Be A Strong Motivator To Seek Mediation

Anger is only followed by aggression in about ten percent of scenarios (Kassinove and Tafrate, 2002). Anger has been proven to encourage you to seek out active behaviours to address scenarios or people you've found problematic but doesn't necessarily mean through confrontation or physical acts. Anger is a strong alert that encourages you to reflect on why someone might be behaving a certain way, and what you can do to restore peace.

3. Anxiety Encourages New Ways Of Approaching Problems And Challenges

When we feel anxious, we'll try and do anything we can not to feel that way anymore. Anxiety is closely linked to our 'fight or flight' response, which allows your body to create energy quickly, ready for action. When faced with dangerous situations, anxiety will take over and encourage us to seek solutions quickly in order to escape danger (Biswas-Diener and Kashdan, 2014).

4. Guilt Helps You Change Negative Behavior

Guilt can be an exceptionally useful emotion. It's essentially our moral compass and when it goes off, it's a good indication that we may have behaved or said something hurtful to someone we care about. It's like our internal system for punishing ourselves when we've done something wrong. People who are more prone to feeling guilty are less likely to steal, do drugs, resort to violence or drink and drive (Biswas-Diener and Kashdan, 2014).

5. Jealousy Motivates You To Work Harder

Jealousy isn't always malicious. Most of the time it's what psychologists refer to as 'benign envy'. Benign envy has been shown to encourage students to perform better on tests and in schoolwork, as seeing another student achieve a good grade made it more tangible for them to achieve too (van de Vien, Zeelenberg and Pieters, 2011). Next time you feel jealous because someone else has achieved a desired goal, try to see this as a good thing – it means the goal is totally achievable for you too.

12.4 Can Negative Enhance Memory Accuracy?

Negative emotions can help improve our memory accuracy. Negative emotions give us mental strength and an experience. Every negative experience give a way of thinking and provide area of decision in future.

12.5 Negative Emotions And Motivation

Arduous life makes us to able solve difficult future problem and prepare for new tough row to hoe so dilemmas are part of life and that are exist in any situation, every time we get the short end of the stick but it is not last and not will be last.

Negative emotion can be utilized to achieve desired goal in life so we should understand our negative feeling.

How Can We Best Control and Deal with our Negative Emotions?

Best plan of attack with our negative emotions is to accept.

The benefits of being happy are enormous, including 1.convalesce 2. prosperity 3. sagacity 4. wellbeing 4. stronger immune systems 5. more work engagement, 6.higher levels of creativity 7. stable marriages and much more.

Negative emotions may be useful indicators of attitude or morality or behavior.

Sims (2017) explored ways to proactively process and acknowledge negative emotions and came up with the acronym TEARS of HOPE to help coach and guide individuals. Here's what it stands for:

T = Teach and Learn

This is the process of listening to what your body is trying to teach you through the presentation of negative emotions, and learn what they mean. It's building your own personal knowledge of the way you respond to emotional states, interpreting the signals your body is sending you, and acknowledging that they serve a purpose.

E = Express and enable

Negative emotions encourage us to express them. They are very actionable emotions. The express and enable part of the acronym encourages you to explore this with openness and curiosity. It's about increasing your acceptance of your natural instincts and enabling them to be present without resentment.

A= Accept and befriend

This follows on nicely from express and enable. It's about befriending yourself and the way you are as a human. Focus on increasing your acceptance with positive affirmations to bring your sphere of negative emotions into a space of acceptance.

R = Re-appraise and re-frame

Once you've begun to accept that this is a natural part of who you are, you can begin to focus on reframing the situation and how you react. Just because a negative emotion has arisen, doesn't mean you have to react in ways that are detrimental to you and those around you.

negative emotions isn't about accepting or excusing poor behaviours, it's about creating awareness for the self and others to create positive reactions.

S = Social support

Knowing that negative emotions are present in all of us, and in pretty much the same way, can be a fantastic source of compassion and empathy to those around us. It's how we process our emotions that differ, so seeing someone in the throws of anger, knowing that they are just handling a perceived threat can really encourage us to approach them with compassion, rather than anger ourselves.

H = Hedonic well-being and happiness

This is the process of grouping positive experiences with negative. Because we more readily recall negative experiences, it can be useful for us to group them with positive experiences so we don't fall into a ruminating trap. This way, we can focus more of our energy on recalling the positive experiences.

O = Observe and attend

Take the time to really observe your reactions without ignoring them, repressing them, or over exaggerating them. Use mindfulness to bring your focus to your mind and body and what a particular emotion is creating within you. Attend to these reactions without judgment.

P = Physiology and behavioural changes

Just as you observe your emotional and mental responses, observe your physiological reactions too. Bring your focus to your breath, your heart rate and sense out the changes in your physiology that a negative emotion may have caused. Again, attend to these changes without judgment.

E = Eudaimonia

This might not be a word you are familiar with, but it's well worth adding to your vocabulary. Eudaimonia is a Greek word which basically refers to having a good spirit. It means you have found a state of being that is happy, healthy and prosperous, and you have learned to engage in actions that result in your overall well-being. It means you're actively striving towards a sense of authenticity in all you do.

TEARS of HOPE

T = Teach and Learn

E = Express and enable

A= Accept and befriend

R = Re-appraise and re-frame

S = Social support

H = Hedonic well-being and happiness

O = Observe and attend

P = Physiology and behavioural changes

E = Eudaimonia

12.6 Envisage Your 'Best Possible Self'

For 30 minute ,we should think about ourselves best possible future & targets and best possible bed future so that we shall prepare for that.Taking the time once a week to practice this can have amazing results on not only your mood but how you approach the scenario next time it comes around.

In a week or month we should commute to think ,what action ,how to take action, why to take action, who will effect by action, where action shall be started, when will tart action.

Time for Self-Reflection

12.7 Practice Gratitude

Practicing gratitude has been shown to have wonderful effects for both the recipients and givers. These effects have long reaching impacts on our mood and perception of events, so it's worth spending a little bit of time adding the practice to your weekly repertoire. Whether it's for a small thing or a big thing, in person, over the phone, a letter or a simple text message, letting someone know you appreciate them or something they have done, can really make a difference in how you perceive and respond to negative emotions.Always response is the key of success and give positive effect on mind.

12.8 Explore Mindfulness Techniques

If you find you have a short fuse and anger is your go-to negative emotion (or if you find you're always on the spectrum of the anger emotion, regularly experiencing annoyance) mindfulness could help to reframe what you're feeling.

Follow the TEARS of HOPE guidance and take the time to understand why you may be responding in this way. Mindfulness can help you find the headspace to do this in a positive way.

12.9 Learn How To Respond Versus React

Do you know the difference between how you respond versus how you react? Negative emotions often encourage us to react immediately to a given scenario. When we feel angry, we may lash out or shout. When we become sad, we may withdraw and reject people around us.

Sometimes we need to act on these impulses, but mostly we don't. By exploring your negative emotions you can start to develop your understanding of how you react, and instead start to switch this to positive ways of responding – which could mean learning that no reaction is required at all.

Know when to take a break

Know when to take a day to yourself. If you are constantly experiencing negative emotions and struggling to manage them, your body is telling you something isn't right.

Take a day to re-center. Fill this day with positive experiences, doing the things that you know fuel you and make you feel good. This kind of break can help to realign your thinking, give you some space to refocus on why you might be experiencing the negative emotions, and come up with some positive coping strategies.

This is just a quick collation of the tips I felt would be most helpful, but it all comes down to you as an individual. Some of them may work really well, and others not so much. Make sure you try out a few different strategies and find the ones that work best for you.

Addressing ruminating thoughts:

1.Try stop quickly if we enter such thoughts.

2.Play games

3.Play with kids

4.Listen music

5.Read or write book

6.Solve puzzles

7.Go outdoors activities

12.10 A Look At Negative Emotions In The Workplace

Our work and the workplace can be sources of great joy and achievement for us. On the flip side, they can also be a battleground for dissatisfaction and a range of negative emotions. These emotions can be doubly troubling at work as we try to manage our reactions in front of professional colleagues and our boss. Failing to do so can result in our job being on the line. I'm pretty sure that's something we all want to avoid!

Below I've taken five of the most common negative emotions that crop up at work and what they might be signalling:

Anger

Anger at work can arise for a number of different reasons. You might be frustrated with a slack colleague, a tyrannical boss, cutbacks or unfair treatment.

Of all the negative emotions, anger is probably the one you most want to keep in check in the workplace. If you feel the familiarity of anger rising at work, remember to respond and not react.

Remove yourself from the scenario by taking a walk and getting some fresh air. Use mindfulness to bring your body and mind back to a state of calm and approach the issue rationally.

Fear

In uncertain times fear can come up at work for a few reasons. You might be worried about redundancy or job security. Or you might feel fear and anxiety because of a toxic boss or colleague. Your fear is telling you that you don't feel safe. Problem solve what is causing your fear and what steps you need to take care to create positive change.

Guilt

Guilt is a tricky one. Maybe you took a sick day when you shouldn't have or blamed a colleague when you missed a deadline. Guilt is your moral compass telling you something is awry. You can't go back and change past behaviours but you can pay attention when the emotion arises and seek to make changes.

Jealousy

Is there one particular colleague who always seems to get the praise? Who may have pipped you for that promotion, pay rise or big client? Jealousy can crop up at work when we feel someone is achieving the goals we want to achieve ourselves but may be having difficulty in doing so.

It's important not to let this become malicious jealousy and steer clear of gossip (unless it's positive) around the water cooler, tempting though it may be. Use your jealousy to motivate you to achieve the goals. Instead of becoming bitter, approach the colleague for advice on how you might be able to improve too. Seek their help and you could form an alliance that reaps benefits, instead of a feud that benefits no one.

Apathy

Feeling disinterested in your work role or tasks is a sign that this needs to be explored. If you're feeling disengaged from your job and colleagues, it could be a sign that it's time to move on or seek new challenges.

No one likes being bored and this could be your passive-aggressive way of sticking your heels in rather than accepting change as needed. If this sense of apathy is spreading into other areas of your life, it could be a sign of depression, so be sure to seek professional support if you're finding it hard to feel motivated about life.

Just as negative emotions outside of work are a sign that something needs to change, the same is true when they occur at work. Explore the feeling proactively and see where it leads you.

In their functional theory of emotion, researchers Keith Oatley and Philip Johnson-Laird (1987), at the Universities of Glasgow and Cambridge respectively, suggest emotions help us choose which goals to pursue, as they act as a barometer for determining the possibility of success when we take a particular approach to a problem.

Frederickson at the University of Michigan and Robert W. Levenson at the University of California, Berkeley (1988), positive emotions also have the capacity to lower physical arousal following some negative event. Consider this simple fact – every bit of software that we use (such as a website) is nothing but a tool, a means to pursue a goal (e.g., to find and purchase a good pair of shoes, or to keep informed of the news of the world). It's not difficult to understand why emotional responses to software can assist us to determine whether we are able to achieve our goals with it, or whether we should look for another bit of software (another website perhaps) that might be more suitable.

The Take Away

We can see that emotions, encompassing both positive and negative emotional states, have the potential to benefit us. And not only can emotions have an enduring and positive effect on our psychophysiology, but they provide us with the impetus to choose and pursue different goal paths. This is of particular importance when an event or situation results in the continual prevention of goal attainment. If we did not experience some negative emotion as a result, we may be more inclined to continue with the same line of attack, resulting in the loss of physical and cognitive resources which are essential for self-preservation.

13. DESIRE

"Every action shall be coherence and resonance with thought. "

A strong feeling of wanting to have something or wishing for something to happen..Within the teachings of Buddhism, craving is thought to be the cause of all suffering. By eliminating craving, a person can attain ultimate happiness, or Nirvana.

Our any acts are triggered by desire. If no desire, than no work will be done by anyone.

Wrong desire is the root of all evils.

Desire may by classify as :-
a. Real :Really required, without it, we cannot live.
b. Pseudo desire: we give logics that are necessary for our life but actually not. For example we someone have lower model car but want another type of car which is not required for that but have logic to explain why is it required.

c. Gratuitous desire: We have no logic but required due to mind hallucination. For example someone purchase a lottery ticket by logic that he want become a rich man.

13.1 Ten Sins

1. Molestation (the act of molesting someone (= touching or attacking them in a sexual way)),

2. Gluttony (over-indulgence and over-consumption of food, drinks, or wealth items, particularly as status symbols)

3. Pluto mania (greed for money or possessions.),

4. Oaf (a man who is rough or clumsy and unintelligent.)

5 Grudge (a strong feeling of anger and dislike for a person who you feel has treated you badly, especially one that lasts for a long time:)

6. Vicious (Vicious people or actions show an intention or wish to hurt someone or something very badly :),

7. Deceit (dishonest behavior; trying to make somebody believe something that is not true),

8. Lynch

9. Brutality

10. Suicide

13.2 Five Virtues

1. Salutation

2. Praise

3. Attentiveness

4. Courteous

5. Discipline

13.3 Five Fortune

1.Long life
2.Healthy life
3.Rectitude
4.Happy life ending
5.Accomplish life goal

13.4 Covetousness

It is strong desire of other's things, which incites us for wrong path. We should see ourselves ability and believe in ourselves what I have is sufficient for me and I am eligible for it only and nothing else.

13.5 Appetite

We should not eat more than enough. The any things that more than enough is not good for us.

13.6 Inclination

 We should not become weak for our desires and become strong against any inclination.

Our desires are our weakness or may our strong point

if it is knowledge so only good reading is the path for ultimate desire.

Life always moving with desires but it should be only for gaining knowledge and no desire shall be our weakness.   Do not keep any secret desires for silent gratification.

14. DEPRESSION MANAGEMENT TECHNIQUES

" True happiness comes when we smile."

There are many ways to reduce depression or sadness in life which all readily available on books or internet. However we will discuss some important ideas here.

14.1 Sun Therapy

We should go outside and walk or relax in sunny day.It is better to go morning and evening to enjoy the sun light. Grazing of sun in morning and in evening, it will give us relax.

we can watch for detail

Sun Gazing with HIRA MANEK

https://youtu.be/D_ERDxxzvQE?
list=PLIvJl3z9A8-4C1LCMoxthXmAfwJULKL25

14.2 Religion Mantra/Verses/Psalm Or

Reading Surahs Or Sing Music As Like

if you follow religious:like Hinduism daily chanting of the Hare Krsna Mantra: Hare Krsna, Hare Krsna, Krsna Krsna, Hare Hare/Hare Rama, Hare Rama, Rama Rama, Hare Hare.
You can read/verse the chapter which give positiveness to your mind.

14.3 Reading Book /Religious Book

Many books available for entrainment as per personal choice may read the books we like. famous book Darkness Visible by William Styron,The Art of Happiness by Dalai Lama and Howard C. Cutler,Ikigai: The Japanese Secret to a Long and Happy Life by Francesc Miralles and Hector Garcia,Think Like a Monk by Jay Shetty,The Practice Of Humanity by Param Pujya Dada Bhagwan,Wings of Fire by A. P. J. Abdul Kalam and Arun Tiwari,Gitanjali Poem by Rabindranath Tagore,The Bhagavad Gita,The Quran,The Bible and many others.

14.4 Learning New Things

We can learn new games, new technology ,new software programming ,new social works or activity ,new tourist interest, new cloth style i.e something new that you enjoy.for example Sudoku, computer programming(C,Python etc),data science ,Artificial intelligence, Mathematics formula ,learn English, Hindi ,Latin, Greek, Russian or any other language ,photography, photo editing ,Automation, play outdoors /indoor game ,play with kids, running, jogging, yoga, medication ,anything we enjoy.

14.5 Watching Video/Movies In Interstate

Watching movie or documentary may relax you so make a list category wise/genre that movies we like. For example :
Comedy:Andaz Apna Apna, Gol Maal, Munna Bhai, Hera Pheri, Padosan (1968), aane Bhi Do Yaaro (1983), 3 Idiots , Chachi 420, Vicky Donor, Namak Halaal, Angoor, Tere Bin Laden,Aankhen etc
English comedy : oliver stoned,Ghostbusters,American pie,Monsters Inc etc
Others Movie: Taare Zameen Par, Oh My God, Dangal, peaceful warrior, Numb, Melancholia, Ordinary People, Dear Zindagi, Anjaana Anjaani, Karthik Calling Karthik, My Name is Khan many more movies we can watch.

14.6 Walking Or Any Physical Activity

Go to your old school or college.Meet to your friends.Do some outdoor activity and enjoy nature.

14.7 Analysing The Problem And Possible Solution

If we have some problem in life,analys the problem in view of 5Wh:
Why:why this problem come.

What:what are reasons of this problem.

Whre:where to go or from where this problem come.

When:when will take a action for solving.

How:How to solve the problem.

14.8 Generate Artificial Happy Environment

Try to happy by artificial environment creation Like neglect real the problem and target the personal achievement or vice versa i.e., run away for time being as there are no solution of problem presently. Problems face not always same every time and has some positive and negative effect and uses. Try to find positive in problems.

14.9 Talking In Cool Way

Way of talking may solve many problems without intervention. Way of talking depend on the person to whom is talking. Logical thinking and Cognition thinking are important parameter to judge the person.

14.10 Love /Empathy With Other

Always love to others don't think negative for others in any situation in spite of what losses has been done by others.

14.11 ERO Rule

If any Event(E) occurred and suitable response(R) has been done then outcome (O) will be always positive. E is not in our control and Outcome (O) may be controlled by taking suitable response (R).So response is the only in our control that control our destiny.Always response positive and appropriate ,logical and in sprit of situation.

14.12 Change Of Air

If we feel bored or depressed or lackluster behavior, we should change our place so that mind feels good and vehemence energy in mind can be instigated. In universe, our Earth is special as we live here. It is not possible to see the world in one life but we can try by seeing as possible new place by visiting.The real knowledge lies in roaming one place to another place.We should visit any new place or known place where we can feel happy.A list of must see place shall be in our mind or in note.

14.13 Make New Friends

If feel loneliness, then try to make friends.Try to Change cloth style ,try to change food, Change self for others.

watch Develop Your Clairvoyance In Less Than 10 Minutes | Guiding Echoes https://youtu.be/nsap-6QO-90?

list=PLIvJl3z9A8-4C1LCMoxthXmAfwJULKL25

14.14 Remove All Negative And No Nega-

tive Self-Judgments :

Everyone has positive and negative attribute so we cannot leave them but we can improve by thinking and determination. Positive thinking can be developed by reading books, watching good movie or documentary etc. Remove all negative things that start thinking you about negativity by neglecting, not follow them. If we think only our targets and nothing more, no negativity will come near to you.

For self ,think positive about your decision and positive self-judgments.we know ourselves better than others.

Some examples are:

1)TED show

You Don't Find Happiness, You Create It | Katarina Blom | TEDxGöteborg   https://youtu.be/9DtcSCF-wDdw

Happiness is all in your mind: Gen Kelsang Nyema at TEDxGreenville 2014 https://youtu.be/xn-LoToJVQH4

Unwavering Focus | Dandapani | TEDxRenohttps://youtu.be/4O2JK_94g3Y

Your health is governed by your Environment | Prof. BM Hegde | TEDxIITHyderabad https://youtu.be/K-mgmIjaRlY

Robert Waldinger: What makes a good life? Lessons from the longest study on happiness | TED https:// youtu.be/8KkKuTCFvzI

14.15 Clap Your Hand And Shake Your Head

Always be happy by clapping and greet to every one only positive words as every thing have only two quality rule "it is good" or "it is very good" and nothing bad exist in universe. Reset your mind by shaking your mind or raucous without thinking of others.

14.16 Change Path

 If you think that your decisions are wrong than immediate change and move to right path. But we should think carefully about changing the path, it may give false result, doesn't worry go ahead you will find your destination. One destination has many paths to reach.

14.17 Always Make Good Relationship With Others

Healthier relationship makes us happier and social connection shall be live always and strongest with others. Strong social connections are important rather than numbers. Love one shall be in healthier and strongest bonding is most important for brain and happiness. Always give importance to good and close relation.

14.18 Depression Due To Time Or Age

It is common for us when we aged feel unsecured and think about what will do for different condition, what will happened? what will do? It is best don't think about and by thinking we wasting our time. We should live in present try to engage in work and make busy yourself. Limit the thinking and plan the things slowly. Think about past and learn about your past decision. For such no discussion required from others if not serious matter.

Life will be enjoyable always in any condition and always will be better.

It may possible presently we are serious problem but be patience and limit with minimum requirement and take anything when opportunities come. Continuous work and monitoring of opportunity and positive thought will take out from problem.

14.19 View Of Who (The World Health Organization)

following points are taken from WHO website:
Living with someone with depression can be difficult. Here are some tips on what you can do to help someone you live with who is depressed, while taking care of yourself at the same time.

What you should know

- Depression is an illness and not a character weakness.
- Depression can be treated. What treatment is best

and how long the depression lasts depend on the severity of the depression.

- The support of carers, friends and family facilitates recovery from depression. Patience and perseverance is needed, as recovery can take time.
- Stress can make depression worse. What you can do for people who are depressed
- Make it clear that you want to help, listen without judgement, and offer support.
- Find out more about depression.
- Encourage them to seek professional help when available. Offer to accompany them to appointments.
- If medication is prescribed, help them to take it as prescribed. Be patient; it usually takes a few weeks to feel better.
- Help them with everyday tasks and to have regular eating and sleeping patterns.
- Encourage regular exercise and social activities.
- Encourage them to focus on the positive, rather than the negative.
- If they are thinking about self-harm, or have already intentionally harmed themselves, do not leave them alone. Seek further help from the emergency services or a health-care professional. In the meantime, remove items such as medications, sharp objects and firearms.
- Take care of yourself too. Try to find ways to relax and continue doing things you enjoy.

Worried that your child is depressed?

Growing up is full of challenge and opportunity–starting and changing school, making new friends, going through puberty and preparing for exams … Some children take change in their stride. For others, adaptation is harder, causing stress and even depression. If you are worried that your child might be depressed, read on.

What you should know

• Depression is an illness characterized by persistent sadness and a loss of interest in activities that you normally enjoy, accompanied by an inability to carry out daily activities, for at least two weeks.

• Additional signs and symptoms of depression during childhood include withdrawal from others, irritability, excessive crying, difficulty concentrating at school, a change in appetite or sleeping more or less.

• Younger children may lose interest in play. Older children may take risks that they would not normally take.

• Depression is both preventable and treatable.

What you can do if you think your child might be depressed

• Talk to him or her about things happening at home, at school and outside of school. Try to find out whether anything is bothering him or her.

• Talk to people you trust who know your child.

• Seek advice from your health-care provider.

• Protect your child from excessive stress, maltreatment and violence.

- Pay particular attention to your child's wellbeing during life changes such as starting a new school or puberty.
- Encourage your child to get enough sleep, eat regularly, be physically active, and to do things that he or she enjoys.
- Make time to spend with your child.
- If your child has thoughts of harming him- or herself, or has already done so, seek help from a trained professional immediately.

Worried about the future? Preventing depression during your teens and twenties

2016-2017

Adolescence and young adulthood present many opportunities – for meeting new people, visiting new places and finding a direction in life. These years can also be a time of stress. If you are feeling overwhelmed rather than excited by these challenges, read on.

What you should know

- Depression is an illness characterized by persistent sadness and a loss of interest in activities that you normally enjoy, accompanied by an inability to carry out daily activities, for at least two weeks.
- In addition, people with depression normally have several of the following: a loss of energy; a change in appetite; sleeping more or less; anxiety; reduced concentration; indecisiveness; restlessness; feelings of worthlessness, guilt, or hopelessness; and thoughts

of self-harm or suicide.
• Much can be done to prevent and treat depression.

What you can do if you are feeling down, or think you may be depressed

• Talk to someone you trust about your feelings.
• Seek professional help. Your local health-care worker or doctor is a good place to start.
• Stay connected. Keep in contact with family and friends.
• Exercise regularly, even if it's just a short walk.
• Stick to regular eating and sleeping habits.
• Avoid or restrict alcohol intake and refrain from using illicit drugs; they can worsen depression.
• Continue doing things you have always enjoyed, even when you don't feel like it.
• Be aware of persistent negative thoughts and self-criticism and try to replace them with positive thoughts. Congratulate yourself on your achievements.

Wondering why your new baby is not making you happy?

Having a baby is a major life event and can cause worry, tiredness and sadness. Usually these feelings don't last long, but if they persist you may be suffering from depression. For more information, read on.

What you should know

• Depression following childbirth is very common. It affects 1 in 6 women who have given birth. Depression is an illness characterized by persistent sadness and a loss of interest in activities that you normally enjoy, accompanied by an inability to carry out daily activities, for at least two weeks.

- In addition, people with depression normally have several of the following: a loss of energy; a change in appetite; sleeping more or less; anxiety; reduced concentration; indecisiveness; restlessness; feelings of worthlessness, guilt, or hopelessness; and thoughts of self-harm or suicide.

- Symptoms of depression after childbirth also include: a feeling of being overwhelmed; persistent crying for no apparent reason; lack of bonding with your baby; and doubt about being able to care for yourself and your baby.

- Depression after childbirth can be treated with professional help. Talking treatments and medicines can help. Some medicines can be taken safely while breastfeeding.

- Without treatment, depression following childbirth can last for months or even years. It can affect your health and the development of your baby.

What you can do if you think you have depression

- Discuss your feelings with people close to you and ask them for support. They might be able to help you look after the baby when you need some time to yourself or to rest.

- Stay connected by spending time with family and friends.

- Get out in the open air when you can. In safe environments, taking your baby for a walk is good for both of you.

- Talk with other mothers who may have advice or be able to share experiences.
- Talk to your health-care provider. He or she can help you find the treatment that is most appropriate to your situation.
- If you have thoughts of harming yourself or your baby, seek help immediately.

Staying positive and preventing depression as you get older

2016-2017

The life changes that come with ageing can lead to depression. To learn more about preventing and treating depression in older age, read on.

What you should know

- Depression is an illness characterized by persistent sadness and a loss of interest in activities that you normally enjoy, accompanied by an inability to carry out daily activities, for at least two weeks.
- In addition, people with depression normally have several of the following: a loss of energy; a change in appetite; sleeping more or less; anxiety; reduced concentration; indecisiveness; restlessness; feelings of worthlessness, guilt, or hopelessness; and thoughts of self-harm or suicide.
- Depression is common in older people but often overlooked and untreated.
- Depression among older people is often associated with physical conditions, such as heart disease, high blood pressure, diabetes or chronic pain; difficult life events, such as losing a partner; and a reduced ability

to do things that were possible when younger.
- Older people are at a high risk of suicide.
- Depression is treatable, with talking therapies or antidepressant medication or a combination of these.

What you can do if you are feeling down, or think you may be depressed
- Talk to someone you trust about your feelings.
- If you think you are depressed, seek professional help. Your local health-care worker or doctor is a good place to start.
- Keep up with activities that you have always enjoyed, or find alternatives if previous activities are no longer possible.
- Stay connected. Keep in contact with family and friends.
- Eat at regular intervals and get enough sleep.
- Exercise regularly if you can, even if it's just a short walk.
- Avoid or restrict alcohol intake and only take medicine as prescribed by your health-care provider.

Do you know someone who may be considering suicide?
Every 40 seconds, someone, somewhere in the world, dies by suicide. For people with severe depression, it is not uncommon to think about suicide.
What you should know if you are worried about someone
- Suicides are preventable.
- It is okay to talk about suicide.
- Asking about suicide does not provoke the act of

suicide. It often reduces anxiety and helps people feel understood.

Warning signs that someone may be seriously thinking about suicide

- Threatening to kill oneself.
- Saying things like "No-one will miss me when I am gone."
- Looking for ways to kill oneself, such as seeking access to pesticides, firearms or medication, or browsing the internet for means of taking one's own life.
- Saying goodbye to close family members and friends, giving away of valued possessions, or writing a will.

Who is at risk of suicide?

- People who have previously tried to take their own life.
- Someone with depression or an alcohol or drug problem.
- Those who are suffering from severe emotional distress, for example following the loss of a loved one or a relationship break-up.
- People suffering from chronic pain or illness.
- People who have experienced war, violence, trauma, abuse or discrimination.
- Those who are socially isolated.

What you can do

- Find an appropriate time and a quiet place to talk about suicide with the person you are worried about. Let them know that you are there to listen.
- Encourage the person to seek help from a pro-

fessional, such as a doctor, mental health professional, counsellor or social worker. Offer to accompany them to an appointment.

- If you think the person is in immediate danger, do not leave him or her alone. Seek professional help from the emergency services, a crisis line, or a health-care professional, or turn to family members.
- If the person you are worried about lives with you, ensure that he or she does not have access to means of self-harm (for example pesticides, firearms or medication) in the home.
- Stay in touch to check how the person is doing.

Do you feel like life is not worth living?
If you sometimes feel that life seems so hard that it is no longer worth living, read on.
What you might be thinking or feeling
- The pain seems overwhelming and unbearable.
- You feel hopeless, like there is no point in living.
- You are consumed by negative and disturbing thoughts.
- You cannot imagine any solution to your problems other than suicide.
- You imagine death as a relief.
- You think everyone would be better off without you.
- You feel worthless.
- You feel very lonely even when you have friends and family.

- You do not understand why you are feeling or thinking this way.

What you need to remember

- You are not alone. Many other people have gone through what you are going through and are alive today.
- It is okay to talk about suicide. It can help you feel better.
- Having an episode of self-harm or suicidal thoughts or plans is a sign of severe emotional distress (perhaps as a result of the loss of a loved one, loss of employment, a relationship break-up, or experience of violence or abuse). You are not to blame and it can happen to anyone.
- You can get better.
- There are people who can help you. What you can do.
- Talk to a trusted family member, friend, or colleague about how you feel.
- If you think you are in immediate danger of harming yourself contact the emergency services or a crisis line, or go there directly.
- Talk to a professional, such as a doctor, mental health professional, counselor or social worker.
- If you practice a religion, talk to someone from your religious community who you trust.
- Join a self-help or support group for people with lived experience of self-harm. You can help each other to feel better.

What you might be thinking or feeling

- The pain seems overwhelming and unbearable.
- You feel hopeless, like there is no point in living.
- You are consumed by negative and disturbing thoughts.
- You cannot imagine any solution to your problems other than suicide.
- You imagine death as a relief.
- You think everyone would be better off without you.
- You feel worthless. You feel very lonely even when you have friends and family.
- You do not understand why you are feeling or thinking this way.

What you need to remember

You are not alone. Many other people have gone through what you are going through and are alive today.

It is okay to talk about suicide. It can help you feel better.

Having an episode of self-harm or suicidal thoughts or plans is a sign of severe emotional distress (perhaps as a result of the loss of a loved one, loss of employment, a relationship breakup, or experience of violence or abuse). You are not to blame and it can happen to anyone. You can get better. There are people who can help you. What you can do Talk to a trusted family member, friend, or colleague about how you feel. If you think you are in immediate danger of harming yourself, contact the emergency services or a crisis line, or go there directly. Talk to a professional, such as a doctor, mental health professional, counsellor or social worker. If you practice a religion, talk to someone from your religious community who you trust. Join a self-help or support group for people with lived experience of self-harm. You can help each other to feel better.

15.SPIRITUALITY

"Humor is good medicine and can actually help keep you in good health."

Pray to God is being by most of us ,purpose of this only happiness in life.In pray ,we sing many spritual song or Bhajan, devoted to God,love with God, pray to God for today and past whatever happened with us.

15.1 Desire And Egoism

if we born then death is real truth and we should not be in sorrow ,it is every one last journy.

Every one in life fighting for their existence ,we also fighting with others but many of them are doing wrong practice they will be out and die one day. with you only are physical health mental health ,and God (God means your good act).Whatever God we follow ,we shall remember every-time in spite of happiness or sorrows if not follow any God with good act, then remember our good act and do every day.Our good act always with us.Nothing is fixed in life ,and when we born countdown start of death.

living being =physical body+soul+act

soul is immortal and act always with soul.any Soul that good or bad is fusion in God and God is infinite. soul is fission from God and create living things.but the process of fusion and then fission is not always follow due to previous act and soul direct rebirth with some decoded information.

we confuse about our duty in life so think deep about self duty.The human being shall do their act rigorously.Without going in real situations,don't runaway from trouble.

Rule of life: There are no rule to live life but certain boundaries are like first I am then other it not means we deprive others ,we should care others also. Ultimate aim of life is not money. All are not same but equal in humanity. Life has certain responsibility ,should take care our responsibility. relation and responsibility bind us with others so we should acknowledge but every things have limits . Our responsibilities are only one way don't expect return gift to other.

Responsibility : Everyone has some fix responsivity because of other responsibilities ,we should return in return of responsibility.

Duties: some responsibilities are our duty ,so return of duties are void so be happy in present.

15.2 Reincarnation

Reincarnation is real truth.The total soul on earth are constant ,only conversion one species to other occurred naturally.Our acts are continuously added for all previous birth.

the question of soul exist

God send you on behalf of him as pro-tempore and act on behalf of him but we are responsible for our every act .the act of Euthanasia and suicide are sin, We cannot take our life in any condition because act pro-tempore or act on behalf of God. Work according the rule of life and probity.

No one with you, only you are responsible for your good or bad act.We always fight in any situation.Every one not sorrows for other or loving death or living things attachment.We should not ego about our color, cast, religion status etc.we should have tolerance or forbear for our trouble.We shall not think about what other thinks, we should do our act continues.don't think about loss/,profit ,lost/gain when doing good act.Doing hard work and think positive for others.our mind shall think only the work or good act.we should practice yoga and mind shall be even or calm.our internal mind will be calm if we leave our desire and anger.we shall be neutral about our happiness or sadness.We shall control or limit our five sense.desire gives anger ,anger gives unbalance in mind.Discipline mind may receive mental stability .Don't be in control of sense.we should not collect money but shall collect good act and don't spent money non essential requirements.we shall leave our ego , possession.By controlling our sense ,we can do good act and may receive happiness.We should do act whole life till death.We shouldn't think only ourselves but also for others.Our health is real wealth so eat healthy and think healthy.

15.3 Depression May Now Be Defined In

Terms Of The Following Attributes

1) A specific alteration in mood: sadness, loneliness, apathy.

2) A negative Self-concept associated with self- reproaches and self-blame.

3) Regressive and self-punitive wishes: desire to escape, hide, or die.

4) Vegetative changes: anorexia, insomnia, loss of libido.

5) Change in activity level: retardation or agitation.

According to major Criteria for depression as following:Depressed mood most of the day, nearly every day, as indicated by either subjective report (e.g., feels sad or empty) or observation made by others (e.g., appears tearful).

b) Markedly diminished interest or pleasure in all, or almost all, activities most of the day, nearly every day (as indicated by either subjective account or observation made by others)

c) Significant weight loss when not dieting or weight gain (e.g., a change of more than 5% of body weight in a month), or decrease or increase in appetite nearly every day.

d) Insomnia or hypersomnia nearly every day

e) Psychomotor agitation or retardation nearly every day (observable by others, not merely subjective feelings

of restlessness or being slowed down)

f) Fatigue or loss of energy nearly every day

g) Feelings of worthlessness or excessive or

inappropriate guilt (which may be delusional) nearly every day (not merely self-reproach or guilt about being sick)

h) Diminished ability to think or concentrate, or indecisiveness, nearly every day (either by subjective account or as observed by others)

i)   Recurrent thoughts of death (not just fear of dying), recurrent suicidal ideation without a specific plan, or a suicide attempt or a specific plan for committing suicide.

15.4 Music Has Color

Music can have a profound effect on both the emotions and the body. Faster music can make you feel more alert and concentrate better. Upbeat music can make you feel more optimistic and positive about life. A slower tempo can quiet your mind and relax your muscles, making you feel soothed while releasing the stress of the day. Music is effective for relaxation and stress management.listening to music change brain functioning to the same extent as medication.Native American, Celtic, Indian stringed-instruments, drums, and flutes are very effective at relaxing the mind even when played moderately loud. Sounds of rain, thunder, and nature sounds may also be relaxing particularly when mixed with other music, such as light jazz, classical (the "largo" movement), and easy listening music.

15.5 Capriciousness Life

There is nothing fix or constant ,everything is changing and nothing is last. Happiness and sadness are always available in life and nothing of them always fix. Happiness and sadness nothing ,they are only perception and understanding of mind ,the solution is only understanding the problem and mental strongness.In real, there is nothing like happyness or sadness ,it is all our mind and felling.

we should practice truthfulness,faithfulness,good act,calmness,knowledge.

15.6 Calmness

Calmness can be achieved by

-Removing our desire

-creating artificial atmosphere by fragrance, flower etc .

-By practice

-By gain more and more knowledge.

-Freeness in life

-store minimum

15.7 From The Gita

Desire is root of unhappiness so get rid of from weed desire. be disciplined for our act and thought. Real happiness is only in self knowledge. Don't expect anything from others only God will give anything you want. Bitter experiences are real happiness because it will give in last some positive result. Thoughts are only the solution of all sadness so belief in you self. All happiness in the materialistic has a beginning and an end, but happiness in Krishna is unlimited, and there is no end. Happiness is only inside us don't search outside world. Free from all thoughts of 'I' and 'mine'.

15.8 From The Bible

We should fear from God for our act. We should grateful to God and every one for their act. We should greet always and all time to others spite of his type of person and feel kindness. Nothing is ours; the owner of everything is God so grateful to him.

15.9 From The Quran

God knows every thing that you are doing good or bad.Always be gratitude which God gives you and God gives you every thing.Do good act and patience for final result and be truthful to your self.Do not transgression of gratefulness of others.Many of us believe in God but when we are in many trouble or series of trouble, we do not believe in God and move to wrong path so it should not be; he is always present for righteous person.Any who lies, will punish by God so be truthful with yourself and others.Don't give false promises.Be away from devious person.Statement should not be averred with confound and dubious, not hide the truth, knowingly.

15.10 Religious Song/Mantra

This may decrease your continuous negative thoughts.

16.FAMOUS PERSONALITIES

"Everyone special for their family and you have quality to be special for everyone."

16.1.Dr. Bhimrao Ambedkar

Ambedkar said in 1935 that he was born a Hindu but would not die a Hindu. He viewed Hinduism as an "oppressive religion" and started to consider conversion to any other religion.From above point of view he was depressed from social status of person and thought about how to uprise such cast deprived person. He took many steps to uprise human kind and social thought.

16.2.M. K. Gandhi

He was famous freedom fighter of India called Bapu .

From livemint.com (https://www.livemint.com/news/world/mahatma-gandhi-s-train-ejection-commemorated-in-south-africa-11623143906557.html):The incident on June 7, 1893,On the fateful night, while Gandhi was on his way to Pretoria from Durban, a white man objected to his presence in a first-class carriage, and he was ordered to move to the third-class compartment.

Gandhi had a valid first-class ticket and refused to obey the orders following which he was thrown out of the train at Pietermaritzburg station. He had stayed at the station that night.he was depressed from special class of reservations in south Africa.After this juncture, he realise the reality of the special class and the common man and started a series of movement which made him a real freedom fighter and synonym of father of nation.

16.3.Jim Carrey

Jim Carrey easily makes the short list of history's most influential comedians, but in an interview with 60 Minutes, the funnyman shocked a lot of people when he acknowledged he has spent much of his life dealing with depression. After the second of his two failed marriages, Carrey sought the help of a psychiatrist who prescribed him Prozac. Though Carrey admits the antidepressant helped him out of an initial jam, he also realized that he couldn't be one of those who stay on the drug forever. "I had to get off [Prozac] at a certain point," said Carrey. "You need to get out of bed every day and say that life is good. That's what I did, although at times it was very difficult for me." Carrey credits a healthy diet and natural supplements for his improved mental health.(https://www.socialworkdegreeguide.com/30-famous-people-alive-today-battled-depression/)

16.4.Lady Gaga

Lady Gaga hasn't been shy about too many things, least of all her long battle with mental illness. In a candid interview with Billboard, the pop star admitted, "I've suffered through depression and anxiety my entire life. I just want these kids to know thatâ€¦" But as you might guess, the "Born This Way" artist has beaten her depression, and has said, "I learned that my sadness never destroyed what was great about me. You just have to go back to that greatness, find that one little light that's left. I'm lucky I found one little glimmer stored away." Today, Lady Gaga works hard as an advocate for mental health. Her Born This Way Foundation seeks to empower youth, inspire bravery, and provide resources for young people dealing with depression, severe anxiety, and even bullying.(https://www. socialworkdegreeguide.com/30-famous-people-alive-today-battled-depression/)

16.5.Sushant Singh Rajput

A newspaper excerpt:
(https://www.hindustantimes.com/bollywood/sushant-singh-rajput-was-admitted-to-hospital-in-nov-doctor-says-he-told-me-he-doesn-t-like-anything-now-doesn-t-wish-to-live/story-ehm3B5GDA-LUfLXoi1xJakJ.html)
he doesn't wish to live and he is afraid all the time. On that, I primarily diagnosed the ailment Sushant Singh Rajput was suffering from to be depression and

anxiety. He told me that he is experiencing these symptoms for the last 10 days," the statement said. However, the doctor added that the actor said during the examination that he doesn't have any suicidal thoughts. He said that from the severity of Sushant's symptoms, he concluded that the actor has been depressed 'for a very long time'.

The doctor had noted that the cause of Sushant's depression was not external. "It was evident from the words of Sushant Singh Rajput, that nothing is happening as per his expectation and that he is insecure. But, the reason was appearing to be negative thoughts in his mind. No strong outer reason was seen for such feelings of his in the examination. Hence, he was a patient falling in the 80 percent grid, as above. Depression can occur to such patients due to thyroid deficiencies, Vitamin B12 & D3 deficiencies, Hemoglobin deficiencies, and imbalance in some chemicals and stimulants in the brain like Serotonin. Some peculiar patients also get anxiety and depression due to heredity," the statement added. Sushant was discharged from hospital on November 30.

Sushant was found dead at his Bandra apartment on June 14. He died by suicide at 34.

16.6.Srinivasa Ramanujan

His interest in mathematics and mad him a profound proficiency in Mathematics but he was not passed in other subject and no other cared about his interest in mathematics and he was depressed about that why he was not reaching his destination and could not play with numbers. He wanted surreal with numbers forever where all numbers around him and wanted to play.. His depression was tool to success and find solution in mathematics.

16.7.Dr. A. P. J. Abdul Kalam

A newspaper excerpt:

After Kalam failed the interview for Air Force pilot in Dehradun---he was 9th and the eight others before him got selected--- in sheer despondence he took a bus to Rishikesh and headed to the banks of the Ganga. That would go on to be one of the most defining moments of Kalam's life. In his words, he "stood at the edge of a cliff with a lake below".This was l957 and his childhood dream of flying a fighter plane had been shattered.

(https://timesofindia.indiatimes.com/city/dehradun/air-force-dreams-down-rishikesh-sadhus-gita-lesson-got-kalam-on-feet-again/articleshow/48256648.cms).

His statement "Two rules for a peaceful life: Depression in failure should never go to heart, and ego in success should never go to the brain."

16.8.Alan García

Alan Gabriel Ludwig García Pérez (23 May 1949 – 17 April 2019) was a Peruvian politician who served as President of Peru for two non-consecutive terms from 1985 to 1990 and from 2006 to 2011.

On 17 April 2019, García died from a self-inflicted

gunshot to the head as police officers under a prosecutor's orders were preparing to arrest him over matters relating to the Odebrecht scandal. He was transferred to a hospital in serious condition, where he remained for more than three hours in an operating room, during which he suffered three cardiorespiratory arrests before his death.

García is considered one of the most controversial yet talented politicians of Peru's contemporary history.He was known as an immensely charismatic orator.

(https://en.wikipedia.org/wiki/Alan_Garc%C3%ADa) From above corruption is main culprit. Integrity, Image of person are important parameter for handle the depression so be careful about Integrity, Image of person.

ABOUT THE AUTHOR

Kamal Kumar Prajapat

Kamal Kumar Prajapat presently is holding a post of gazetted officer in Indian Railway . He had qualified UPSC Engineering Service Exam -2009 then in Indian Railway with different buckle down positions like Deputy Chief Plant Engineer (Junior Administrative Grade)/Rail Coach Factory Kapurthala Punjab, Deputy Chief Electrical Engineer(Railway Electrification, Ahmadabad, Gujarat) ,Assistant Electrical Engineer(Asansol) ,Divisional Electrical Engineer(Malda (West Bengal) and Bhagalpur(Bihar)) .He also had work exposure in Hindustan Aeronautics Limited(H.A.L.) ,Nasik- Maharashtra and college education teaching. He is M.Tech (IIT BHU Varanasi, UP) & B.E (University College, Rajasthan Technical University formally Govt. Engineering College Kota Rajasthan) withal enrolled for Ph.D in IIT Madras but dropout. He has published some Technical Papers in IEEE also. He has experience in the field of administration, Railway coaches maintenance, Railway Electrification.

"Words Power","Practice Book Class 1 Mathematics (Addition)" are another books for advance English learner and kids.